GENDER
AND
UNIVERSITY
TEACHING

SUNY Series in Gender and Society

Cornelia Butler Flora, Editor

GENDER
AND
UNIVERSITY
TEACHING

A
NEGOTIATED
DIFFERENCE

Anne Statham
Laurel Richardson
Judith A. Cook

State University of New York Press

Published by
State University of New York Press, Albany

© 1991 State University of New York

For information, address State University of New York
Press, State University Plaza, Albany, N.Y., 12246

Production by M.R. Mulholland
Marketing by Dana E. Yanulavich

Library of Congress Cataloging in Publication Data

Statham, Anne.
    Gender and university teaching : a negotiated difference / Anne
Statham, Laurel Richardson, Judith A. Cook.
        p.   cm. — (SUNY series in gender and society)
    Includes bibliographical references and index.
    ISBN 0-7914-0703-9 (alk. paper). — ISBN 0-7914-0704-7 (pbk. :
alk. paper)
    1. College teaching—United States—Evaluation.   2. Women college
teachers—United States—Rating of.   3. Sex role—United States.
4. Sex differences in education—United States.   I. Richardson.
Laurel. II. Cook, Judith A., 1955– .   III. Title.   IV. Series.
LB2331.S693 1991
378.1'25—dc20   90-44786
                                                                      CIP

10 9 8 7 6 5 4 3 2 1

Contents

Contents

Tables and Figures

Acknowledgments

Many individuals have contributed to this project through the years. First, we thank the professors who gave freely of their time, allowing themselves to be interviewed and us to enter their classrooms. Without their willingness to participate and trust in our process, we never could have proceeded. They also gave us access to student evaluations. We thank the students, also, for answering our survey. Second, we thank the Graduate School at Ohio State University and the National Institute of Education (Grant G–78–0144) for funding this project; we especially thank our program officer at N.I.E., Susan Klein. Others assisted in various stages of this project in ways that included reading and reacting to the manuscript, giving counsel on our observation method, and making observations. They include Mary Margaret Fonow, Connie Gaib, Jack Hough, Joan Huber, Lisa Koogle, Elizabeth Madsen, Bettye Pfau-Vicent, Kath Schoemaker, Sheldon Stryker, and Barrie Thorne. Amber Ault and Dianne Small provided an enormous amount of assistance in the final stages of the project. Special thanks go to Michael Zupan, Ernest Lockridge, and Dennis Grey for support and encouragement throughout the project. Finally, we wish to say that we have all made equal contributions to this project and, so, consider ourselves to be equal co-authors.

Acknowledgments

Theoretical Approaches to Understanding College Teaching

Every autumn, at colleges throughout the nation, a rustle is felt on the campus as faculty members, both male and female, put aside unfinished manuscripts, grant proposals, studies, and leisure to prepare for teaching. For some faculty members the students are a bother; having to meet classes is a gross imposition on their time. For others, teaching is a necessary task that pays the bills and provides some measure of personal gratification. For still others, the autumn rustle is one of excitement because teaching is the core of their lives; they can't wait to get back into the classroom.

For nearly all university faculty members, teaching is a salient activity. Male and female professors think about their teaching, interact with students, and are evaluated by those students. Whether it is abhorred, tolerated, or welcomed, teaching affects professors' use of time and energy, and has potential consequences for job retention and promotion. University teaching is also an important issue for society more generally in view of the alarm that has been sounded concerning the current "crisis" in undergraduate education. Several authors have written about this problem in recent years (Bloom 1987; Hirsch 1987), discussing in great detail the supposed erosion of our post secondary system. Although much of this literature focuses on failings in the curriculum, a substantial portion stresses the need for renewed concern with the teaching process itself. The need for "good teaching" (Bennett 1984), for "a new partnership approach" with students is emphasized (Upcraft et al. 1989). Yet, despite the importance of teaching for society in general and for the university professor in particular, little systematic attention has been paid to some essential aspects of this situation. We may gain important insights by looking at such features as gender similarities and differences in how teaching is perceived and managed, and whether students evaluate male and female professors differently. This study explicitly addresses these issues: What do male and female professors say about their teaching? What do male and female professors actually do in their classrooms? How do students evaluate their male and female professors?

In examining gender differences in teaching styles, we draw upon several theoretical perspectives. The tradition in the social sciences is to construct competing explanations based upon several theories and to search for the most robust explanation, declaring that theory to be "the best." We take a somewhat different approach, however; we begin with the assumption that each of several theories may offer complementary insights into the situation and that each may account for part of our findings, helping to give us a more complete picture.

Our thinking about gender and university teaching evolved in stages; successively we incorporated more advanced thinking about gender as it operates in our society, drawing from developments in the social sciences more generally. When we began to design this study, the literature on sex roles was dominated by the structural role theory paradigm, wherein individuals are assumed to occupy roles or positions with fairly fixed or immutable expectations; the influence of social structure was thought to be primary. Because role expectations were regarded as so unalterable and because individuals occupy many roles simultaneously, much of the research in this tradition dealt with the problem of role conflict. Researchers in this area spent a great deal of time exploring methods for dealing with this conflict—compartmentalizing, setting priorities, and so on. Originally we approached our topic in this way, believing that women professors likely would experience a great deal of conflict between two often opposing roles: female and professor. Because of society's generally negative (and immutable) view of the female role, we also believed that women professors would have difficulty being accepted as competent. We believed they might be caught in a double bind, rejected either for being female (not professorial) or for being professorial (not female).

This approach was fruitful; we did find evidence of these problems, as have other researchers who observe women professionals. Yet, we also discovered that the situation is much more complex. As we began to analyze our data, we were influenced by emerging and changing views of gender, views that reflected elements of symbolic interaction role theory. Although symbolic interactionism has long existed in sociological thought, it has been incorporated only fairly recently into the literature on gender roles. This perspective focuses less on the structural, immutable, generalizable role expectations that exist across situations and more on the extent to which these expectations are continuously renegotiated and reaffirmed in the process of interaction. In analyzing this microlevel, the level of interpersonal interaction—change rather than stability—becomes more apparent. Role players have the option, indeed the agency, to modify role expectations; they are not faced with totally immutable demands.

By incorporating this perspective into our explanatory framework, we have been able to account for our findings more fully than by using either perspective alone. After all, both processes operate in social life. We face structural pressures, but we can decide whether to accommodate to those pressures, or to negotiate with our role partners to reject them outright or to modify them in part.

The influence of symbolic interaction role theory is seen in the feminist literature on the contextual view of gender roles, which stresses the negotiation process, and in the woman-centered literature, which emphasizes taking the woman's view. Both principles—the importance of negotiation and subjective reality as determinants of social life—are the essential underpinnings of the entire symbolic interaction framework. What follows is an examination and synthesis of these perspectives; in the process we will show how feminist theory can contribute to a mainstream sociological theory such as symbolic interactionism, as well as draw from it.

The Situational Parameters of University Teaching

University teaching traditionally has been considered a male activity; it became even more male-dominated during the first half of this century than previously (Roby 1973). Obviously, it is also a middle-class pursuit in which rationality, logic, and reasoned arguments are preferred, even presumed, and in which emotions and feelings are suppressed, devalued, even presumed absent. Because what is valued in the university has been regarded traditionally as masculine in our culture (Addelson 1983; Cook and Fonow 1984), women may well be at a disadvantage in this context. (But see Shor 1980 for possible differences in community college, working-class environments.) Indeed, many studies document the discrimination that women in academe have experienced (Astin and Bayer 1973;

Roby 1973). In part, it is argued, the difficulty stems from stereotyping on the part of students (Basow and Silberg 1985) and colleagues (Hall and Sandler 1982), which has caused women professors to be evaluated as less effective despite equivalent levels of professional performance.

Women confront similar stereotypes when entering other male-dominated professions (Ward and Grant 1985); barriers to women's success in the professions have long been recognized (cf. Epstein 1970). For example, women physicians are reported to be under strong pressures to outperform male physicians (Brown and Klein 1982); women lawyers find it exceedingly difficult to attain levels of "concrete" success similar to those of their male counterparts (LaRussa 1977); women in health care management face lowered (though improving) odds against mobility (Weil 1986); and women professors still face major hurdles (Theodore 1986). These difficulties persist even though women professionals are well prepared for professional life by the influence of significant others (Lunneberg 1982), show motivational levels similar to men's (Kaufman and Fetters 1980), have improved their publishing records (Mackie 1977), and manage to avoid tedium and burnout despite higher levels of job stress (Pines and Kafry 1981).

Part of the perceived difficulty for women arises from the conflicting expectations experienced by women in academe. These women are expected to demonstrate both female and male sex-typed behaviors—to be simultaneously "warm" and "logical," for example. This conflict is especially strong, it is argued, because the larger context, the university, is male-centered (Langland and Gove 1981). These conflicts have been described and documented by Huber (1973) and by Schwartz and Lever (1973), among others. Managing these conflicting expectations might increase a woman's strain on the job and might decrease her chances for advancement within the academic hierarchy.

From this evidence we would expect the context of the university classroom to call forth and reinforce traditional sex role stereotypes as they exist in the broader society. Other evidence, however, suggests that this might not be the case. Attaining a university professorship is a true mark of distinction that can override normative expectations for gender-appropriate behavior. Such an accomplishment imbues the woman with a certain amount of authority and power that is not ordinarily present in our sex-graded society. The extent to which a woman can use these attributes successfully to negotiate acceptable and empowering self-definitions and to convey them to her colleagues and students will affect the extent to which these role partners value her. Recent considerations of women's use of power suggest that women are capable of breaking through "control myths" (the common understandings that define women as powerless) in order to operate effectively in powerful positions (Lipman-Blumen 1984), although the precise patterns of the use of power may vary in different situations and may differ from those observed among men (Baker-Miller 1982; Gordon 1985). A woman in a powerful position in relation to students—that is, a university professor who has the ability to influence those students' behavior by virtue of her position—may be granted legitimate power—authority—by those students.

Several pieces of evidence suggest that the trappings of the immediate context, the professorial role, may well outweigh stereotypical gender roles in influencing actual behavior. For instance, certain studies (Babladelis 1973) show that students have similar expectations for men and for women professors. Historically, highly educated women have been used to demonstrate the inaccuracy of myths about women's limitations (Beard 1946) and to serve as evidence for the claim that gender is a potentially variable phenomenon. Hence, teaching in higher education may obviate traditional gender role expectations (Bernard 1964). The fact that both men and women face the constraints and expectations of a middle-class culture that places a high premium on intellectual functioning might negate the traditional expectations that women be passive, dependent, and primarily nurturant. Indeed, the passive, intellectually subordinate professor might appear "deviant," regardless of sex. The following sections explore these ideas more fully, relating them in detail to earlier empirical work as well as to theoretical explorations. In subsequent pages we will detail how we have come to construct an argument based on the two versions of role theory—normative and interpretive (Wilson 1970)—with emphasis on the contextual/woman-centered perspective and on the centricity of relationships to women's teaching styles.

Theoretical Perspectives

Earlier Perspectives

Structural role theory, the earliest of these theoretical positions, has generated considerable sociological and communications research. According to this theory, individuals play many roles and possess different statuses simultaneously (cf. Goode 1960; Merton and Barber 1963). Because particular behaviors are associated with particular statuses, males and females are expected to act differently. This perspective presents a view of highly bifurcated, segmented roles, abstract in their expectations and interpretations (cf. Tresemer 1975). It is seen most clearly in the status inconsistency/role conflict research and in certain areas of the earlier research on communication styles.

Status inconsistency/role conflict. In the structural perspective on roles and statuses, individuals are perceived to hold clearly demarcated roles that often call for competing behaviors. Hence, not only are male and female roles perceived to exist in dualistic opposition to one another, but such dualism also is perceived to exist within individual lives. This perspective holds that all individuals play many roles and possess different statuses simultaneously. Often the roles carry conflicting expectations and the statuses have conflicting prestige. Supposedly, these conflicts are problematic for individuals; one cannot possibly perform two opposing behaviors at once (Goode 1960; Gross, Mason, and McEachern 1966; Merton and Barber, 1963), nor can one respond simultaneously to two widely divergent prestige attributions (Goffman 1957; Jackson 1962; Lenski 1954). A great deal of research has been directed at documenting the supposedly adverse effects of these conflicts on the individual (cf. Burchard 1954; Gross, Mason, and McEachern 1966; Jackson 1962).

Women professors, a distinct minority, are thought to face two types of potential conflict: (1) role expectations for females (warm, nurturant, supportive, nonassertive; cf. Lewis 1972; McKee 1959; Sherriffs and Farrett 1953) conflict with the expected behaviors of the university professor (directive, assertive, knowledgeable); (2) the university professor is given a fairly high prestige rating in contrast to the low prestige attached to the sex status of female (Hodge, Siegel, and Rossi 1964; Mischel 1974). Thus, difficulties arise for the woman professor in the form of both role conflict and status inconsistency. The mode of resolving these conflicts is crucial. Whether she resolves the conflict along gender-stereotypic or gender-innovative lines, such resolution might create secondary problems. For example, if she adopts a male-typed teaching style, she might be resented strongly by her students; if she adopts a female-typed teaching style, she might be judged incompetent. Such a situation represents the classic double bind (Bateson 1960). Men are not expected to experience this double bind (cf. Babladelis 1973;

Bernard 1964; Graham 1978; Schwartz and Lever 1973d; Wikler 1976). Consequently, according to structural role theory, a woman's teaching experience will differ qualitatively from that of her male colleague.

Although recent evidence suggests that professional women in general and academic women in particular have made great strides in managing the tension between the personal and the professional and between femininity and competency (Gray 1983; Williams and McCullers 1983; Yogev 1983), previous evidence suggests that a double bind exists. It was perceived to exist, for example, among the women interviewed by Wikler (1976). These women professors described painful dilemmas in which they were either resented by students for lacking "femininity" or undervalued and perceived as incompetent for lacking "masculinity." Ferber and Huber's (1973) study of more than 1,000 undergraduates at a large Midwestern university found that both male and female students preferred male teachers.

Communication patterns. A second body of earlier research, the literature on communication patterns, suggests that women professors might encounter teaching difficulties. Some of this literature posits the existence of consistent sex differences in behavior. According to this research, female-typed behavior patterns are likely to incur judgments of incompetency, even when the women's actual contribution is as great as the men's (Eskilson and Wiley 1976). Men are judged to be more competent in part because of their use of "power" speech (O'Barr 1984; Thorne 1979), which includes such male-typed strategies as giving directions, offering opinions, interrupting others (West and Zimmerman 1983), and referencing oneself as an authority. Women, on the other hand, are found to use disempowering speech tactics such as waiting for someone else to state ideas and then agreeing with them strongly, rather than introducing ideas. Women also make a larger proportion of supportive conversational utterances such as "uh-huh" and "mmm" and, generally, aid the conversational success of others at their own expense (Fishman 1977). Indirect means of making contributions to the group result in lower competency ratings by group members, even though the women often have as much influence as the men on the group's eventual decision (Eskilson and Wiley 1976). Other studies yielded similar results (Meeker and Weitzel-O'Neill 1977). More recently, West (1982) has found that women's contributions continue to be devalued regardless of the communication style they use.

Some evidence on elementary and secondary school teachers suggests that these gender differences in communication apply to the teaching situation. Whereas men teachers are more achievement-oriented, more concerned with communicating ideas, more authoritarian, and more likely to give corrective, sharply critical feedback, women teachers give more positive feedback, encourage and receive more contributions from students, and refer continuously to students' ideas when elaborating or making a point (Brophy and Good 1974; Frazier and Sadker 1973; Good, Siber, and Brophy 1973; Griffen 1972; Lee and Wolinsky 1973; Moore 1977). Some of these findings also have been observed at the university level. Male students were found to make and receive more comments in classes taught by males, whereas both sexes participated and were attended to equally in female professors' classrooms (Karp and Yoels 1976). Thus, men may adopt a more aggressive male sex-typed style, which emphasizes their competency, whereas women may adopt a more nurturant female sex-typed style, which deflects attention from their expertise in the subject matter (by making extensive use of students' contributions in the learning process).

In general these perspectives lead us to expect that women will adopt a defensive management strategy, attempting to "cool out" students' resentment of their authority and competence while trying at the same time to establish that authority. The net result would be a great deal of stress for the woman professor as she deals with pressures that men professors do not have to face. Perhaps she must demonstrate competence and mastery of the subject matter in a particular way in order to reduce students' resentment and to simultaneously enhance her authority.

Both men and women professors are affected by students' expectations, at least to some extent. After all, demonstrating successful teaching is an important requirement for retaining an academic position (Martin 1984). Evidence of this success is based in part on students' evaluations. Therefore, any behavior pattern that systematically elicits negative responses from students will seriously harm professors' chances of job retention. Several types of expectations are important. Some involve judgments of competency; most professors strive to appear competent. A related dimension is hostility. Even if students evaluate positively women professors who use behaviors expected of competent men, they might resent women professors for placing them in an uncomfortable and normatively stressful position. Their ensuing hostility then would magnify the woman's discomfort about her ambiguous position and thereby would increase her anxiety, a state that lowers job performance in a myriad of settings.

Further, and more subtly, because the professorial role includes a research and service component, the greater time and energy that the female professor gives to managing her teaching role will reduce the time and the other resources available to her for fulfilling other requirements for tenure. Consequently she might find job retention more difficult than her male colleagues.

One possibility suggested by these arguments is that women professors might encounter job strains that their male counterparts do not experience. The deck may be stacked against women, reducing their chances of professional success. Thus, even though women are allowed entry into these high-level positions, their work setting might not be equitable in demands on time or energy—not because the institution is discriminating but because women face the additional tasks required to deal with normative ambiguity and with the accompanying reactions that their presence in academia creates. We also might expect students' reactions to reflect this double bind. For example, students might prefer women who use female-typed approaches but might regard these same women as less competent than men.

Interactionist Role Theory

In recent decades, emphasis has shifted away from viewing role behavior as a process of enacting prescribed roles to focusing on the creation of new roles through interpretive role taking. This more interactive approach assumes that actors themselves define a social situation and that congruence of these definitions enables efficient and organized behavior (Stryker 1959). Roles are not simply enacted; they are created and continuously modified. Through defining the social situation and anticipating how others will respond, actors can create and modify conceptions of their own roles and the roles of other actors (cf. Stryker and Macke 1978; Stryker and Statham 1985; Turner 1962; Turner and Killian 1972). Thus, in any social situation, the self and other role definitions are likely to shift, requiring concomitant adjustment on the part of all participants (Blumer 1969). When confronted with conflicting role requirements, the actor can choose which sets of expectations to honor; intentional creation of a third role and the unintended emergence of a new role are also possibilities (Turner and Killian 1972). In our analysis we view this plasticity in role definitions and behaviors against a background in which roles are said to be interrelated in three principal

ways: (1) in the person, (2) in interaction, and (3) in the social structure (Turner 1975). Here we focus on understanding how role definitions are negotiated and portrayed at these three intersecting levels
of social experience. Moreover, we focus on understanding how individuals come to create, redefine, and maintain role relationships.

At the individual level, interactionist versions of role theory
focus on the individual's psychological adjustment to and acceptance
of roles and role relationships. Moving away from the notion of inter-
nalization, for example, the interpretive framework considers individual reactions and accommodations to the emotional dimensions
of role experiences (Turner 1975). Also acknowledged are individuals' freedom to bring role portrayals into line with personal preferences (Stryker and Statham 1985) and the notion that this personal
accommodation changes over time as actors "grow into" their roles
(Thornton and Nardi 1975). This acknowledgment of the self as an
important motivator of behavior recognizes that demands come
from internal as well as external sources.

A second level of the interpretive approach, that of social interaction, traditionally has been the focus of ethnomethodologists, who
seek to uncover the actors' interpretive rules for dealing with a
typified world (Cicourel 1970; Garfinkel 1972; Schutz and Luck-
mann, 1973). This approach contains the important insight that
unequal distribution of power between role partners influences the
ways in which the interpretive process is carried out (Pfohl 1975). As
a result, one actor's resistance to the interpretation and negotiation
of another becomes a focus for those trying to understand the outcomes of the role-taking process (Daniels 1967; Douglas 1970). Interaction with role partners also is acknowledged as an important early stage of the process by which actors adjust psychologically to their
roles (Thornton and Nardi 1975). Moreover, attempts to engage in
role alignment with one's role partners are accomplished as both
partners enter into a testing, probing, negotiating process that occurs during interaction (Stokes and Hewitt 1976). From this perspective, a broadly viewed role such as gender affects the allocation
and performance of other roles, ultimately influencing the extent of
"role-person merger" or the acquisition of role-appropriate attitudes
and adherence to the role in the face of more advantageous roles
(Turner 1978).

Social structure is a third level of the interactionist perspective. As Turner states:

> A woman nurse has been more likely to be *perceived as a per-
> son through her occupational role* than a woman in business

and *a woman elementary school teacher* more than a *woman professor*, if our inference is correct (1978, 11–12; emphasis ours).

Thus, for the actor and for his or her role partners, the possession of other roles and their structural societal importance condition the extent to which the actor identifies and is identified with a particular role, especially "master roles" or "statuses" such as gender. Structure is also important in the formulation of Hewitt and Stokes (1976), who argue that while negotiating new role arrangements actors must reaffirm cultural ideals in order to ease tension and to allow role stabilization. Thus, even when redefining roles innovatively, an actor must pay lip service to the old ways of perceiving the role, to its obligations, and to the societal values that underlie it. Our theoretical synthesis, then, must recognize the structural overlay of certain primary roles that influence the portrayal of additional roles in the actor's role constellation. According to this perspective, women professors are seen as freer than men to discount sex-stereotypical behavior and freer to be innovative performers of the professorial role, but not free to dismiss totally the underlying cultural ideals about "femininity" or the obligations that underlie them. Women professors, then, could diverge considerably from female sex-stereotypical behavior but still would be restrained by it.

The Contextual/Woman-Centered Perspective

The contextual nature of gender. Elements of this interactionist tradition are seen in the contextual and woman-centered views of gender, which we call the contextual/woman-centered perspective. The contextual component reconceptualizes gender itself, viewing it as a "variable variable" and not as a set of rigid traits and behaviors inherent in the individual (cf. Broverman et al. 1970). One behaves differently according to the specific demands of the situation. From this newer perspective, gender is regarded as a continuously constructed social identity (Gerson and Peiss 1985) that can be separated from sex both conceptually and empirically (Gerson 1985). Because gender identities are socially constructed, the immediate social context is undeniably salient (Thorne, Kramare, and Henley 1983). Moreover, because sex and gender are distinguishable and distinct, men in certain situations display behavior traditionally thought of as "feminine," and women in certain situations display behavior traditionally thought of as "masculine."

Evidence exists to suggest that gender behaviors and attitudes are far from universal, even within ostensibly the same culture. For

example, recent evidence suggests that gender differences in communication styles are not nearly as pervasive or as all-inclusive as
suggested by earlier findings (Thorne et al. 1983). In fact, certain
characteristics formerly regarded as true only of women's speech,
such as tag endings, have been found in some situations to be more
prevalent in men's speech (Dubois and Crouch 1977; Johnson 1980;
Lapadat and Sessahia 1977). The differences that do exist may be
reinterpreted not as reflecting weakness but as demonstrating wom-
en's attempts to "build rather than contest, share experiences . . . do
interaction work" (Thorne, 1983, 8). These strategies might be quite
effective in the context of teaching.

A great deal depends on the context in which individuals must
function, on the social actors involved, and on their perspectives and
preferences. From this perspective, the assertion of the more traditional view that rigidly distinct and separate gender worlds exist (cf.
Rosenberg 1982) is regarded with suspicion. Such a perspective "can
easily revert to innatist assumptions and separatist solutions" (Bandarage 1983, 14). Although gender differences in approaches to many
of life's activities are acknowledged to exist, the immediate social
context is a variable condition that creates deviations from the expected pattern. This perspective, then, drawing upon major compo-
nents of interactionist theory, accounts for instances when gender
differences *fail to appear*. From this standpoint we would seek an
explanation in overriding aspects of the immediate social context,
for just as surely as gender colors our enactment of other roles
(Turner 1978), other features of our social setting color our enactment of gender roles. The failure to consider these other features
might account for the apparent contradiction in the literature cited
above concerning the existence of role conflict for women professors;
some studies confirmed its existence, others did not. In our study we
consider the impact of professorial rank (assistant, associate, full
professor) as a mitigating feature of the social context; role conflict
may be less pronounced among women of certain ranks.

Taking the woman's perspective. Another, more recent approach argues that researchers need to take the woman's perspective, both to expand our knowledge and to explore male biases in
social theory (cf. Eisenstein 1983). This approach emphasizes the
interactionist notion of the actor's perspective, recognizing that different social groups and even individual actors or role partners will
view a single phenomenon quite differently. If research is to be
meaningful for women, it must make women the center of inquiry.

Taking a contextual, woman-centered approach focuses on women's interpretations and experiences and relates those experiences to ongoing social structures and values that affect women's choices and chances. This body of work focuses often on the theoretical useful-ness of women's own interpretations of their experiences, as well as on the implications of these interpretations for women's empow-erment.

Stanley and Wise (1983), for example, start from the premise that women's experiences constitute a separate ontology or way of making sense of the world. Their notion of a female world of mean-ing, grounded contextually in women's experiences, recognizes sim-ilarity in form but wide variation in content and expression of wom-en's consciousness. Their emphasis on the importance of routine, mundane, taken-for-granted aspects of women's everyday lives ac-knowledges that experiences at this level help to perpetuate female subordination and argues that changes must address this sphere.

Similarly, Dorothy Smith (1979) proposes social analysis *for* women, not *about* women. Her method involves starting with the situation of the woman as she finds herself, focusing on her practical activities within her social context and from that point reconstruct-ing the meaning she derives for her life. Smith's approach allows the investigator to study social relations within the very contexts orga-nized by these relations and to examine reflexively how properties of social relations are incorporated into the analytical and interpretive procedures used by the investigator. By doing so, Smith argues, we come ultimately to findings that can and will be useful to women's empowerment.

Illustrations of this new perspective include Richardson's work (1985) on the "other woman," the single woman involved in a long-term affair with a married man. By grounding her findings in her respondents' everyday lives and interpretations, Richardson was able to understand these women's motives and the definitions of their hidden relationships and could discover similarities in the de-velopmental histories of these liaisons. She came to recognize the positive aspects of the affairs as well as the constraining features. In a similar vein, Cook's work (1988) on mothering the chronically men-tally ill used the context of the enormous practical and emotional burdens facing women who care for psychiatrically disabled off-spring. By focusing on these women's own definitions of mothering their sick children, Cook showed how one could understand mater-nal behavior beyond the "overinvolved" or "schizophrenogenic" mother stereotypes. Equally as important, her analysis explained how a contextualized, empathic understanding of mothers' behavior could be integrated by clinicians attempting to support women who care for our large deinstitutionalized population of mentally ill. Likewise, Statham (1987) studied women managers from their own viewpoints, discovering a unique and unrecognized management model in the process. Again, a negative view of women (incapable of managing) was corrected; new management models were explored and articulated.

Other proponents of the woman-centered perspective focus on the changed assessment of women, per se, arising from the analysis. A final key consideration is that women's styles and strategies should be evaluated on their own terms, not as deviant from or inferior to men's styles and strategies (cf. Belenky et al. 1986; Eichler 1980; Fishman 1978; Gilligan 1982). The female style is not judged deficient or inadequate; rather, the strengths and weaknesses are evaluated in a given situation. Women's ways are viewed simply as a different strategy to achieve the same goals. For example, Gilligan (1982) reexamined Kohlberg's (1963) study of the development of moral reasoning and showed that young girls were classified erroneously as less well-developed morally than young boys because they were using a different set of criteria to determine appropriate behavior in a given situation. Men, she argued, would act from an ethic of autonomous decision making and a search for the existing higher moral order. Women would address the impact of any decision on existing relationships and on the well-being of the individuals involved. Who is to say that one approach is superior to the other? They are simply different. Had Kohlberg recognized this point, his classification scheme certainly would have been more complex. Findings from other studies reinforce this difference between men's and women's basic orientations. Belenky et al. (1986) find that women prefer a more "connected mode of learning" than men. Rubin (1983) finds that women desire closeness and connection in intimate relationships, whereas men value autonomy and fairness. Some of these differences also are seen in children's play patterns (Thorne and Luria 1986).

Whereas Gilligan's framework has been the subject of recent critiques (cf. Auerbach et al. 1985; Greeno and Maccoby 1986; Kerber 1986; Stack 1986; Luria 1986), her response to these criticisms (1986) underscores points relevant to our analysis. Critics of Gilligan state that a woman-centered analysis may result in a dangerous oversimplification (Kerber 1986), which exaggerates rather than illuminates gender differences by reifying stereotypes about women (Auerbach et al. 1985; Luria 1986), such as women's reputation for attributes like altruism and empathy (Greeno and Maccoby 1986). The methodology we employ, however, allows us to discover whether such differences exist and also permits us to look more closely at situations where gender divergence is *not* apparent. Moreover, incorporating this woman-centered perspective into the analysis provides the possibility of presenting in our study a new moral or normative voice regarding university teaching. Like Gilligan (1986) we see this possibility as outweighing difficulties with and objections to the perspective. As Smith has argued, one attempts to give a voice to those "deprived of authority to speak, the voices of those who know society differently" (1974, 12). Thus the perspective alerts us to the goal of "reworking cognitive styles (p. 146) . . . naming and legitimating a female-centered inquiry" (p. 142) (Swoboda and Vanderbosch 1984).

The woman-centered perspective also warns us not to disassociate women's experiences with their thinking in the analytic process (Gilligan 1986, 327). Given this ontological commitment in our approach to teaching styles, we focus on what women do, how they feel about it, and how students, colleagues, and others react to it, as well as the relationships among these different aspects. This emphasis on the grounded nature of women's experiences focuses on their actual activities while simultaneously taking account of the women's own reactions, their interpretations of their own and others' attitudes and behavior toward them, and how all of these influence and are influenced by the reactions of others.

Underlying woman-centered research is the implication that women's behavior has been studied and interpreted (misinterpreted) from a male-centered perspective. To document women's behavior truly, without androcentric value judgments, the observer must forsake the deficit perspective that takes all typically female behavior to be problematic or less valuable than males' behavior. Working from the woman-centered perspective involves recognizing that women's approaches may represent strengths, not weaknesses. Several researchers make this argument specifically concerning women's teaching styles (Richardson 1982; Fisher 1982; Wikler 1976). In our research we consider how women professors' styles of teaching may be equally valuable as men's styles.

A Unified Perspective

This study and its interpretations are guided by an integration of the various theoretical perspectives presented previously. First, we accept the concepts of role theory as informed by inter-actionism—the notion of shared gender role definitions, existing alongside conflicting gender role expectations—and we recognize that actors work out individual solutions in the course of interaction.

In addition, various insights from the feminist theories discussed above inform our application of interactionist role theory, enhancing its explanatory power in accounting for women's experiences. Of critical importance is the concept of the *relationship*, embodying the notion of bonding or connection (cf. especially Gilligan 1982). Much recent feminist writing includes this concept, the notion that connection—caring about and tending to relationships—distinguishes men's lives from women's in a radical, basic manner. Women are assigned the task of tending to personal relationships while men tend to the "public realm." (See Eisenstein 1983 for an elaboration of this idea.) Hence, theories constructed to account primarily for men's experiences typically ignore the centricity of caring and connection. Indeed, the view of the *relationship* as an underpinning for much of social life is expressed in such well-known feminist sayings as "The personal is political."

Role theory, even interactionist role theory, is lacking here. Although this formulation is based upon the notion of reciprocity (which by its very nature entails a relationship), it has not focused explicitly on the relationship as a powerful motivating force for individuals. The implications of the relationship, the degree of attention paid to it, actors' concern with variations in its quality, and ways in which the enactment of new roles are filtered through it are of central importance to women, but these themes have seldom been explored systematically in role theoretical literature. For the most part, this traditional theory has held the *self*, the *individual*, to be the prime motivator for social action. Subjective reality, reflected appraisals, and many of the classic concepts in this perspective from Mead and Cooley to the present day have been concerned with self-judgments and self-presentations. Significant others are important for the feedback they give us about our selves; role partners confirm or call into question self-images. This list of applications is endless, and all concern the individual. Feminist theory emphasizes the relationship—the concern with and the attempt to maintain certain types of relationships—as the primary motivator for social action.

This insight allows us to see the tremendous complexity of the situation, as shown by Mead, but with an additional layer that he ignored: our gender-typified social world, how it is perceived and approached by the two sexes, and how the relationship actually may be an important motivator of behavior for many social actors. The importance of "perspective," of the definition of the situation, thus becomes heightened. It can affect basic approaches to social life, making one theoretical formulation less relevant for certain groups.

As for our own study, understanding the importance of the relationship to this process may help us to account more fully for the behaviors we see among men and women professors, and for how students respond to any existing differences or similarities. It is not only one's sense of self that guides the process of role negotiation and role conflict resolution, as discussed previously by interactionist theorists (Stryker 1980). Certainly the self is a vitally important concept. Equally important, however, and perhaps more so for the study of women's behavior, is the notion that individuals influence their social environments by creating certain types of relationships with role partners that emphasize caring and concern for the nature of the interpersonal bond; they are motivated to behave in certain ways because of their concern for that bond.

Belenky et al. (1986) found that women in academic settings are more comfortable with learning environments that enhance their personal power rather than imbue them with some higher authority stemming from their dissemination of knowledge, *and* that permit an integration of knowledge with their personal experiences rather than requiring that they suppress those experiences. In view of these findings we might expect women to attempt to provide that type of learning environment for their own students. They could accomplish this goal by forming relationships with students that encourage them to bring their personal experiences to the classroom and empower them as independent, autonomous learners. Certainly this effort might lead to the formation of relationships more personal than men professors find comfortable and would cause more personal experiences to be incorporated into the learning/teaching process.

We come now to a major insight. We propose that the woman professor's ability to create a classroom atmosphere where relationships can be formed and can influence learning will determine in large measure her ability to negotiate the complex array of competing role expectations that she faces: the demands that she be both feminine and professorial, personally likable and competent. We expect that her concerns with connection and with nurturing these relationships will not serve as ends in themselves but will become the mechanism for accomplishing the task at hand, namely teaching effectively. Further, we expect this strategy to be especially pronounced among women at lower professorial ranks (assistant and associate professors), who are most involved in establishing their professorial identities and with negotiating competing role expectations. We anticipate that more senior professors, at later stages of role acquisition, will mold the professorial role more often to fit their own personal needs.

Thus, we add another level to the argument that combinations of factors in particular situations might cause role enactment to change. For example, as faculty members advance through the ranks from assistant to full professor, they become more professionally confident and less dependent on others' immediate feedback to confirm their occupational identity as a professor. If Thornton and Nardi's (1975) formulation is valid, the developmental process of role acquisition becomes more and more internal to the individual over time. Thus, the nature of the role might change for established faculty members. Specifically, if actors become more secure in their roles the longer they hold them, tenured faculty may come to feel freer to violate any of the role demands found to exist for men and women professors in general.

A developmental view of roles. In the literature on both structural and interpretive role theory several investigators have noted that actors' role performances and definitions change over time (Thomas and Biddle 1966). Not only is role performance assumed to improve with practice the longer an individual enacts a role (Cook 1984); time is also a factor in negotiating new role attributes, in the "alignment" of roles with those of other actors, and in the societal requirements for role stability (Stokes and Hewitt 1976). By taking a developmental perspective on role acquisition, for example, Thornton and Nardi (1975) detail a series of stages in an actor's psychological acceptance of and conformity to new roles. These stages move from an initial anticipatory stage where adjustment to the role begins, through a formal stage guided by role partners' expectations, into an informal stage in which the actor's own role expectations assume central importance, and finally into a personal stage during which actors modify roles to fit their internal personalities and psychological needs.

Such a perspective is relevant to our study in light of the nature of our academic sample. By including women and men at three career points—assistant professor, associate professor, and full professor—we can examine the developmental issues that arise for men and for women in the process of acquiring the role of university faculty member. Men and women might appear more similar at some points in their careers and more divergent at others. Shifts in the power relationship between a professor and students, for example, also may occur over time, changing the leverage of each party in influencing the role performance and role bargain (Goode 1960). In view of evidence that university women are concentrated at the lower ranks, such as assistant professor, instructor, and graduate teaching assistant, a look at those women who have ascended their university's academic hierarchy will reveal how professorial women's views of their roles and students' reactions are related to academic rank.

Summary and Predictions

This study can be seen as an important empirical test of several recently developed sociological theories of gender relations. These theories stress the variability of gender, the importance of the immediate social situation in determining gendered behaviors, and the importance of taking the woman's perspective in an attempt to avoid androcentric valuations of women's behaviors. These theories, based upon an interactionist version of role theory and role conflict resolution, combine the notion of negotiated social order with the insights into structural sources of role conflict offered by the historically dominant structural version of gender role theory. In our analysis we integrate the insight from feminist theory regarding the importance of the relationship for women's behaviors with the principles contained in traditional structural and interactionist role/status inconsistency theory to enhance the explanatory power of these more traditional approaches. Thus, we offer a test of recently emergent theory *and* a way of integrating theoretical innovation into the mainstream of sociological thought.

Gender Differences in Teaching Approaches

The structural version of role conflict/status inconsistency provides valuable insights into the differences that can exist between men and women professors; from this perspective we derive the concept of the double bind. The interactionist version of role conflict/status inconsistency emphasizes the negotiation process that occurs between role partners. Thus it helps us to account for similarities we might find (i.e., men and women can negotiate to behave in less stereotypical ways in certain situations) and also to explain the existence of gender differences in teaching that are accepted with relative ease by everyone involved (again, negotiations with role partners can lead to such acceptance).

The new feminist theories of gender provide us with the mechanism for resolving the conflict predicted by structural role theory, namely negotiation of the role relationship. We can arrive at this insight by taking the woman's perspective, by attempting to understand what the woman is trying to accomplish with her behaviors, and by examining the immediate social context of the bond itself. From this standpoint we expect women professors to create certain types of relationships with their students that allow them to execute their teaching functions in a way that is acceptable both to their students and to themselves.

Student Responses

With respect to students' responses, the structural version of role conflict/status inconsistency predicts that a double bind exists, such that women professors who use a female-typed style will be liked for doing so but at the same time will be judged less competent. From this perspective, when role demands are viewed as immutable, the woman cannot win; she will be either disliked or judged less competent.

From the interactionist perspective, including the newer theories dealing specifically with gender, we argue that gender differences are negotiated in the course of interaction and can have quite positive effects on role partners. According to this perspective, strengths exist in women's approaches; at the very least, students will accept both strategies (to the extent that differences exist) as equally appropriate and effective. In fact, students actually may *expect* men and women professors to differ in certain ways, and may even reward them for doing so. We have the data to test these different notions.

Feminist Pedagogy

Our predictions about women's teaching behaviors bear a strong similarity to the styles espoused by the feminist pedagogy model. Feminists using this model seek to empower students (Schuster and Van Dyne 1985) by sharing the power of the professorial role with students (Freedman 1985; Shrewsberry 1987; Weiler 1988). The goal is to build a collaborative relationship in which students become self-directed learners (J. Fisher 1987).[1] Cooperative learning using a democratic process is the norm (Schniedewind 1987;

Shrewsberry 1987). Students often have input into the structure of a course (Bright 1987; Maher 1985). Some feminist professors see their role more as "consultant" or "clarifier" than as a typical authoritative professor (Omolade 1987). In addition, feminist pedagogy places emphasis on integrating personal experiences (subjective knowledge) and on dealing with affective reactions to the material being presented (Dunn 1987; B. Fisher 1987; Thompson 1987). Many adherents believe that women learn most effectively in this way; they cite Belenky et al.'s (1986) study as evidence. The integration of personal experiences into the classroom is intended partly to enable students to analyze their situations more effectively. As such, "Every woman is a potential theorist" (Thompson 1987, 81), capable of analyzing her own and others' experiences. To accomplish these ends, the professor must use the interactive teaching style most frequently; lecturing is kept to a minimum. Insofar as our expectations are confirmed—namely that women in general, who might not identify themselves as feminists, use this approach more often than men—we will show that feminist pedagogy itself is based directly on the experience of being female in this society.

We turn now to a description of the study: its setting, the sample, the instruments, and the variables we examined. We discuss the methodology at some length because we used both quantitative and qualitative methods; some readers might be more familiar with the qualitative, others with the quantitative. Our methodological approach gave triangulation an integral role in seeking a theoretical synthesis drawing upon standard sociological perspectives as well as feminist approaches. Next, we look empirically at three teaching issues: basic instructional behaviors, authority management in the classroom, and personalizing. Following that, we examine students' reactions to the teaching styles of the professors whose classrooms we observed. We conclude by evaluating the different theoretical perspectives and by discussing their vision of a theoretical synthesis that explains our findings most clearly.

The Study

University teaching is historically a male activity; the faculty club, a male province. The cultural expectations of the university context—rationality and logic, distance and objectivity—have been associated with "masculinity" rather than "femininity." In such a context we might expect that women professors would be greatly disadvantaged in their teaching, judged by male standards; perhaps they would be found wanting, simply by virtue of being women and by eliciting sex-stereotypical responses. Alternatively we might argue that a woman's attaining a professorship at a research university is such a mark of accomplishment that she is imbued with the prestige and authority of the position, and that this authority overrides traditional sex-role expectations.

Nowhere is this cultural context of academia stronger than in the research-oriented Ph.D.-granting institutions of higher learning. For this reason we chose a large Midwestern state university as the research setting. The university has major graduate programs, professional schools, and research centers as well as a large undergraduate enrollment. The university expects excellence of its professors; demonstration of competence in research and teaching are requisite to tenure, although research excellence clearly receives greater weight in promotions, salaries, and perks. If male and female professors differ significantly in their teaching attitudes and behavior in this somewhat rarefied academic atmosphere, it is likely that gender affects teaching on other campuses as well.

To discover sex differences and similarities in what professors say about teaching, what they do in the classroom, and how students evaluate them, we devised a triangulated research design that integrated quantitative and qualitative data. We *interviewed* professors through semistructured and open-ended questions about their teaching. We *observed* professors teaching in the classroom; for this aspect of the study we used the Hough and Duncan time unit method, by which we coded, at five-second intervals, twelve different dimensions of teaching behavior. We *surveyed* students about their reactions to the professors we interviewed and observed. We obtained observational and student survey data from a sample of 167 professors and their students; we obtained the interview data from a (largely overlapping) matched subsample of thirty professors. Assistant, associate, and full professors from male-dominated and nonmale-dominated departments in the sciences, the humanities, and the social sciences were included in the study. Hence, we have information based on observations of actual behavior in the classroom, on professors' perceptions of and attitudes toward teaching, and on students' evaluations.

A triangulation approach such as this provides several research advantages because it can "exploit the assets and neutralize, rather than compound, the liabilities" (Jick 1983, 138) of different data collection methods. The basic premise of triangulation is that the weaknesses of a particular method are compensated for by the strengths of other methods; qualitative and quantitative methods are viewed not as competitive but as complementary. If data collected through different methods converge, greater confidence in the results is generated (Denzin 1978, 291). In addition, the use of multiple methods is particularly well-suited to integrating or synthesizing different theories. This procedure is of interest to us because the methodological logic parallels the theoretical logic, specifically the concern with bringing diverse perspectives to bear on a problem (Campbell and Stanley 1963; Denzin 1978).

The Setting

The setting for the study was a large Midwestern state university in an urban setting. Most undergraduate students are state residents; approximately one-fourth come from the local county. These characteristics of the university and of the student body should be kept in mind when we discuss our findings about teaching styles because the styles may be unique to large universities with a high proportion of local students.

Related to the size of the university is the size of the classes. Many classes contained nearly 100 students; the average class size in our sample was approximately fifty. Although the effect of class size can be controlled to some extent in our analyses, it cannot be removed entirely because even if students have some smaller classes, their classroom behaviors will be influenced by their typical classroom experience. Hence, the subjects in our sample may exhibit behaviors, such as lower student responsiveness and more lecturing by professors, that are not found among their counterparts at other types of institutions such as small liberal arts colleges.

These features, however, should not invalidate our gender comparisons, which are the primary focus of the study. On the contrary, we can make such comparisons only by looking at men and at women professors in similar situations; otherwise, any apparent gender differences might be the result of situational factors. Possibly, some commonly held assumptions (e.g., women are more strongly committed to teaching) are at least partly the result of the different institutions of higher learning in which men and women are likely to be found. Women Ph.D.s, who are employed more often at small teaching colleges (Astin 1973), might be more committed to teaching only when they work at these small colleges. Excellent teaching is often a prerequisite for retaining jobs at such institutions. Women at large research-oriented institutions, such as the university studied here, might be no more dedicated to teaching than men in similar institutions. Our data will shed some light on this possibility.

The particular setting used for this study is ideal for another reason: women Ph.D.s might have the most difficulty establishing themselves as competent in the heavily research-oriented climate of such institutions. This setting also might present the most stringent challenges to women if they have greater propensities for establishing personalized connections between students and professors. Hence, this setting will likely afford the best test of how gender influences teaching styles.

As stated, our research design called for three distinct data-gathering processes. We observed professors teaching their classes; we interviewed professors about their teaching, and we surveyed students about their reactions to the professors we observed and interviewed. These methods represent not only variations in technique but also a broad, eclectic approach to the entire research enterprise. Each technique—observation, interview, and survey—is based upon a well-articulated philosophy underpinning social science research. Essentially we are blending a grounded, qualitative approach with a structured, quantitative approach. In view of the extent to which these two approaches are commonly considered to be polar opposites, we were impressed with the extent to which findings from the two approaches were complementary; each approach informed and elaborated what was learned from the other. Whyte recently reported a similar strategy in one of his projects; this experience led him to conclude, "Reliance upon a single research method is bound to impede the progress of science" (1984, p. 149). In our study we derived noteworthy benefits from the triangulation strategy. The fact that all three sources of information pointed to similar conclusions increased our confidence that our findings did not result from some idiosyncrasy in applying a particular methodology. Multiple sources also added to the richness of our theoretical insights.

Although there are different ways to analyze teaching, we chose to focus on three main categories: basic instructional activities, authority management, and personalizing. Each is an important aspect of teaching activity as well as a category in which considerable differences in style can be manifested. For *basic instructional activities* we analyzed what professors said about their goals, preparation, and teaching concerns. We coded "basic instructional" behavior in the classroom, specifically professors' attempts to communicate subject matter clearly (structured presentations) and their attempts to include the students (participatory learning). For *authority management* we asked professors how they managed inattentive, disruptive, and disrespectful students. We observed how they managed their authority in the classroom and coded authority-legitimating techniques such as giving evaluative feedback, reprimanding, and interrupting. For *personalizing* we analyzed interview materials concerning how professors felt about students, their willingness to listen to students' problems, and their feelings about socializing with students. In the classroom we coded instances of acknowledging a student by name, sharing personal information, empathizing verbally with students, and incorporating students' lives into the learning process.

The research permits us, then, to specify similarities and differences between male and female professors' beliefs and behaviors in three major teaching categories. Further, the design of the research permits us to examine how rank, disciplinary orientation, and departmental sex ratio are associated with male and female professors' teaching styles.

Whether gender is a factor in how professors teach, however, is a different question from whether students have different expectations of male and female professors and consequently evaluate them differentially. We look at students' evaluations of professors along two dimensions: competency and likability. Is the professor judged competent? Is the professor judged likable? By surveying students from the same classes we observed, we assess which teaching behaviors are associated with students' evaluations of male and female professors' competency and likability. Do students prefer gender-differentiated teaching styles? Are women rewarded or punished for deviating (if they do so) from male teaching styles? The research permits us to answer these questions.

The Sample

Observation Sample

To obtain a sample of classes for observation and students' evaluations of university professors, we designed a sampling procedure that would yield equal numbers of men and women in male-dominated and non male-dominated departments. Our goal was to obtain a sample of 160 professors; the final sample was 167. We were concerned about representing male-dominated and non-male-dominated departments equally in our sample for several reasons. First, because of the popular notion that subjects taught in male-dominated fields (e.g., physics and chemistry) are more "objective," permit less student participation, and require more control by the professor, we wanted to be certain that this effect was not confounding any gender differences.

In addition women in male-dominated departments might differ from other women because of their token positions (Kanter 1977). In particular, women in these departments might feel even more status anxiety than other women; any support networks on which they could draw in their work setting would be heavily male. Their students might have more stereotypic or more denigrating expectations of women than students in other departments. For all of these reasons we wanted both sexes from both male-dominated and non-male-dominated departments to be represented equally in our sample. Moreover, on the basis of Kanter's (1977) work showing the negative impact of occupying a token position in an organizational unit, we wanted to be able to control for male domination of department in our analyses.

We defined a male-dominated department as one whose tenure-track faculty was composed of 80 percent males or more. On the basis of information provided by the affirmative action officer in the university, we decided that the 20 percent cutoff point would provide the best numerical distribution of departments into male-dominated and non-male-dominated categories while maintaining a meaningful substantive distinction. Other researchers have used similar criteria (Hesselbart 1978; Sternglanz 1979). Actually, only a few non-male-dominated departments contained as few as 20 percent women; most were more than 33 percent female.

We excluded several types of departments from consideration because they were inappropriate for our study. These included departments where the professor's communication was largely nonverbal, such as art, physical education, and dance; we eliminated foreign language departments because of obvious difficulties in observing such classes; and we eliminated professional schools that included no undergraduate teaching component because we believed that the undergraduate teaching experience would affect profoundly the styles and strategies developed by professors.

After we made these eliminations, the male-dominated departments were accounting, anthropology, astronomy, biochemistry, botany, chemistry, classics, computer science, economics, environmental education, engineering mechanics, law, horticulture, geography, history, management sciences, mathematics, philosophy, photography and cinema, physics, political science, psychology, and zoology. The non-male-dominated departments were black studies, communication, comparative studies in the humanities, English, family and human relations, history of art, home economics education, home management and housing, human nutrition and food management, linguistics, social work, sociology, and textiles and clothing.

After classifying the departments, we selected several to serve as the major source of professors. These were the larger departments, which represented a cross-section of different disciplines. The male-dominated departments chosen were chemistry, economics, engineering mechanics, geography, history, horticulture, mathematics, philosophy, physics, and zoology; the non-male-dominated departments were black studies, communication, comparative studies, English, family and human relations, home management and housing, human nutrition and food management, sociology, and textiles and clothing.

We sent letters and consent forms to all full-time tenure-track faculty in these departments, asking them to participate in a study of teaching styles. Our goal was to obtain forty men and women professors in both male-dominated and non-male-dominated departments (160 total) who were teaching targeted classes during the two quarters of observation. We obtained almost enough men by this method; 36 percent of those who received letters met our selection criteria and agreed to participate. Yet although 49 percent of the women we contacted met our criteria and agreed to take part, we fell short of the sampling goal for women, primarily because the target departments contained so few women faculty members. Consequently we sent letters to the women in the other potential sample departments, asking them to participate. Nearly 44 percent of these women agreed to participate. Because so many faculty members at this university do not teach undergraduates or are in "research positions," and because professors are notorious for resisting observation while teaching and for reluctance to make their student evaluations available to outsiders, we considered this participation rate acceptable (table 2.1).

The sample we obtained reflects fairly well the rank distribution of faculty in the university (table 2.2). We slightly oversampled male assistants and undersampled male associates and full professors; however, the differences are not statistically significant. Notice that this sex difference in rank distribution is not explained entirely by differences in the age distributions. Men are slightly older, but not nearly so much older as the rank distributions would lead one to expect. Apparently women in this university, as in most universities, have moved up the ranks more slowly than men.

On the whole, our sample of professors is probably somewhat younger than the total population. Perhaps younger professors are more deeply involved with their teaching (as shown in later chapters) and thus are more likely to participate in the study. Obviously we were less likely to receive cooperation from those who were uncomfortable or unconcerned about teaching, so our sample may be especially unlikely to include poor or totally uncommitted teachers. Consequently our sample probably is more representative of average to good classrooms in the university and of professors who are

TABLE 2.1

Sex and Male Domination of Departments of Men and
Women Professors in Sample

	Male-dominated[a] Departments	Nonmale-dominated Departments
Sex		
Females	31	40
Males	57	39

[a]At least 80 percent of department faculty is male.

TABLE 2.2

Rank and Age[a] of Sample and Population, by Sex

	Females		Males	
	Sample	University	Sample	University
Rank				
Assistant	61.2% (43)	63.3%[b]	24.6% (23)	36.2%[c]
Associate	23.9% (17)	25.7%	34.1% (33)	27.4%
Full	14.9% (11)	11.0%	41.3% (40)	36.4%
Age				
20–29	18.3% (13)	—	7.3% (7)	—
30–39	42.3% (30)	—	38.5% (37)	—
40–49	19.7% (14)	—	32.3% (31)	—
50–59	19.7% (14)	—	17.7% (17)	—
60+	00.0%	—	4.2% (4)	—

[a]The university data on age were not available.

[b]Chi square = .3108 for difference of proportions, p > .10

[c]Chi square = 3.64 for difference of proportions, p. > .10

more, rather than less, confident in their pedagogy. Our sample is almost entirely white; four professors were black and one Hispanic, yielding proportions consistent with the nonwhite faculty population.

Interview Sample

In order to examine university professors' attitudes and perceptions about their teaching, we selected a purposive sample of fifteen full-time regular female professors, primarily from the larger sample, and matched them to fifteen male professors on rank (assistant, associate, full), disciplinary orientation (humanities, social sciences, natural sciences), and sex ratio of department. The logic behind the sampling was to control for other variables such as stage in career, discipline, and departmental sex ratio, which might explain differences in experiences and strategies. That is, we selected the interview sample so that we could discover whether women professors, regardless of rank, sex ratio, and disciplinary orientation, reported similar experiences, faced similar problems, and employed similar management strategies or whether other variables such as rank, discipline, and sex ratio context overrode the saliency of sex. Hence, we selected a female and a male professor at each level (assistant, associate, full) from the natural sciences, the male-dominated humanities, the non-male-dominated humanities, the social sciences, and the female-dominated disciplines.

In constructing the matched sample we were concerned about the problem of self-selection; we assumed that professors who agreed to be interviewed would be better teachers, while those who refused would be poorer teachers. This expected bias in our sample did not appear, however. Students' evaluations of professors who were interviewed varied widely in regard to judgments of both likability and competency. In addition, because every professor who was contacted agreed to participate (a 100 percent response rate), no one was self-selected out of this sample. Of course, some self-selection might already have occurred in drawing the interview sample from the observation sample.

We attempted to match men and women within specific departments whenever possible. Because most departments had relatively few women faculty members, female professors were selected first, and male professors were matched to them. In matching for female-dominated departments we employed the opposite strategy: we selected men first because they were less numerous. Unfortunately not every professor who was interviewed was also observed. Matching specifications required us to select from outside our observed sample in three instances (two men in a female-dominated department and one woman in a science department).

Methods

The methods we used in this study were predicated on two primary research principles: first, that triangulation, or the use of different methodologies in understanding any given social activity, is the preferable strategy, and second, that the *particular* research question should dictate the methodology used rather than vice versa. Consequently we used primarily a qualitative approach to examine what professors say about their teaching, and primarily a quantitative approach to learn what professors do in the classroom and to see how students responded to their teaching. We describe first the methods used for the interview sample and then those used for the observation sample and for students' responses.

Interviews

We conducted semistructured, open-ended interviews with thirty professors in order to elicit qualitative material on several issues: (1) general attitudes toward teaching, (2) perceptions of students' expectations for male and for female professors, (3) perceptions of what constitutes basic instructional activities, (4) management of authority, (5) and perceptions of personalization. We probed these areas in terms of professors' experiences of role strain, the strategies and tactics employed to reduce role strain, and the perceived costs and benefits of that strain (see appendix D for the interview protocol).

We were interested in knowing what professors would say about their teaching, both for its intrinsic value and as it related to the observational and survey data. The open-ended format permitted respondents to give accounts based on their own definitions of the situation and to introduce new topics rather than merely respond to the researchers' preconceived categories.

As with any subjective self-report method, the veracity of the interviewees is not known. Yet if we may judge from the rapport established during the interviews ("I want to know how other women (men) manage," "When can we see your results?" "Do *other* professors experience this?"), from the direct presentation of information that was personal and potentially damaging (particularly for the untenured), and from the structure of the interview, which permitted faculty to volunteer material rather than to react to our conceptions, we see little reason to question the credibility of the material. The interviews were conducted in the faculty member's office and were tape recorded and transcribed. Most of the interviews lasted from one to two hours. Two of the researchers, who had considerable research interviewing experience, conducted the interviews. In reading the transcripts three judges were unable to distinguish which interviews were conducted by which interviewer.

Analysis. The transcripts were subjected to a content analysis by the two researchers who conducted the interviews. We used the "constant comparative method" (Glaser and Strauss, 1967) of qualitative analysis to develop indicators for basic instructional activities, authority management, and personalizing. Thus, we obtained qualitative material on professors' views of themselves as teachers (which may or may not have corresponded to their actual classroom behavior) as well as professors' perceptions of their students' needs and attitudes (which may or may not have conformed to the students' actual judgments).

Indicators of basic instructional activities emerged; these tapped the salience of the teaching role for our respondents as well as their endorsement of participatory learning. Specific indicators included their attitude toward teaching, the amount of time they spent preparing for class and discussing classroom episodes, their involvement in teaching, and their desire for students' input and evaluations. Indicators of authority management issues included the extent to which students challenged the professors' authority, the strategies used by the professors to deal with these challenges, and other problems with authority and role distance. Indicators of personalizing included the amount of chatting with students before and after class and the kinds of personal information that the professors and students shared in and out of class. (The indicators are described more fully in the chapters dealing with each dimension).

Each interview was analyzed separately by the two interviewers. We resolved differences by discussing the criteria for each category, although such differences rarely occurred, even with the more complex indicators (see chapter 3). After the transcripts were coded, the two researchers conducted independent analyses of sex, rank, discipline, and sex-ratio variations that were evident in the coded data. Once again, interpretations were cross-checked for consistency between the researchers.

In reporting the results of the qualitative analysis we used illustrative quotations from the interviews; these quotations represent a dominant or general theme. In order to preserve our respondents' confidentiality we omitted some parts of the professors' statements and substituted our own words in brackets or used ellipses. This step was necessary because many departments contained only one or two women at associate and full ranks, so that identification would have been easy.

Observations

We obtained information on teaching style with a modification of Hough and Duncan's (no date) direct observation method. Professors were observed in their classrooms by trained observers, and their behaviors were organized into the three areas of interest: basic instructional activities, authority management, and personalizing.

The principal investigators and the research staff were trained by an expert, who subsequently consulted with the staff in adapting the Hough and Duncan system to our particular purpose. We elected to use a version of Hough's method, itself a variant of the Flanders technique (Duncan and Biddle 1974), because it yields fairly objective data. Because this is a time-unit method of observation, it does not require high-inference coding on the part of the observer; instead, it requires the coding of activities that occur in each five seconds of class time. Thus, it does not depend upon highly subjective ratings based on the observer's impression. For a subject such as ours, about which many cultural stereotypes exist, we desired a highly objective measure. The observers might have expected women to be more supportive or more permissive regarding students' input, for example, and so might have perceived this difference to occur, whereas a careful count of the amount of time spent in these activities may have produced quite different results. With this approach we obtained accurate baseline data about what actually was happening in these classrooms.

Many experts criticize high-inference observation techniques because of their subjective nature and suggest the use of more quantitative, objective methods instead (Duncan and Biddle 1974; Rosenshine and Furst 1973). Admittedly, the method we used yields discrete information, thus causing some researchers to question its ability to capture the holistic nature of the classroom. We attempted to compensate for this by asking our observers to record certain impressions of the classroom immediately after the coding session. We believe that the gains made in obtaining more objective data in this part of the study far outweigh the loss in holistic impressions because the baseline data were very important for the later analysis and for theoretical integration.

We used an observer coding method rather than videotape or tape recording to ensure as much as possible a normal classroom process uninterrupted by the observer. This method is quite appropriate for use with university professors. In fact, it was used successfully to document the teaching styles of recipients of distinguished teaching awards on the campus where the study was done.

The adapted version of the Hough-Duncan technique. The observation method codes all classroom behaviors into twelve basic categories, which include such behaviors as thinking, laughing, initiating, responding, and judging correct or incorrect (see table 2.3). These categories also could be modified with what are called "subfunctions" and "subscripts," a process that provides more complete and more complex information about what occurred. For instance, we could state that a certain basic category, such as responding to a student, was a particular kind of behavior, such as an admonishment or an unspoken communication. Then we combined measures into indicators of the three general concepts we wished to tap: basic

TABLE 2.3

Basic Categories of Behavior Coded with the Modified
Hough-Duncan Technique

1. Thinking
2. Laughing
3. Manipulating others
4. Initiating or presenting information, directions, etc.
5. Responding to questions, solicitations, etc.
6. Soliciting clarification
7. Soliciting in general
8. Judging a contribution to be correct
9. Judging a contribution to be correct using personal criteria
10. Acknowledging another's contribution
11. Judging a contribution to be incorrect
12. Judging a contribution to be incorrect using personal criteria

Note: For a fuller explication, see appendix A.

instructional activities, authority management, and personalizing (see Appendix A).

Data collection. To collect these data, one or more of our trained observers attended what the professor had designated previously as a "typical" class session. We avoided observing atypical sessions such as visits from guest speakers, instructional films, group presentations by students, examinations, and examination pre-test and posttest reviews.

Classroom coding began with the ringing of the bell or the beginning of the professor's giving attention to the class as a whole. The classroom process was encoded for the entire 48-minute session unless circumstances such as late arrival or a delayed start by the professor prohibited it. In *no* case was encoding carried out for less than 45 minutes, and in no case was this reduction deemed significant for our research. Classes that met for longer periods were encoded for only 48 minutes, from the beginning of the class period.

Observers attended classes as scheduled by an administrative research assistant, who was not a member of the observer staff. All follow-up contacts required after the initial contact to obtain consent were made by this nonobserver assistant. Therefore, subject professors had no contact with observers before the observed class session. Classes were allocated among the observers by a system of mutual agreement within other time constraints; no systematic allocation of classes involving a specific gender, academic department, time of day, and so on was made to any one observer.

Observers' reliability. Multiple observers periodically encoded the same class to provide reliability checks. Interobserver reliability remained at acceptable levels (greater than .80) throughout the study. Also, an analysis of variance checking for observer effects (see appendix B) showed that no serious differences existed. Hence, we are confident that our observations yielded valid results.

Measures. We constructed measures in the three areas of conceptual interest: basic instructional activities, authority management, and personalizing. Each measure gives the proportion of classroom time spent on a behavior or on certain clusters of behavior. Observers recorded classroom behavior in five-second intervals, recording a symbol for a given behavior when it began and making tally marks for each five-second interval in which the behavior continued. Consequently we have an accurate account of five-second intervals in each class period and of what was occurring during each interval. If behavior changed during a five-second interval, the new behavior was coded. We have no way of knowing exactly how few seconds such behaviors lasted, but because this situation was so rare, we do not regard it as a problem. To construct our measures, we simply summed the numbers of all classroom behaviors recorded for each observation (including all tally marks).

Observers' impressions of classroom atmosphere. In addition to observing and coding behaviors during the classroom period, the observers also recorded whether the professor tended to: (1) remain stationary or to move around during class, (2) maintain or not maintain eye contact with the students, (3) talk extemporaneously to the class or to rely almost exclusively on notes, (4) include discussion in the class format or to use only a lecture presentation, (5) create a casual classroom climate or to maintain a formal atmosphere, (6) use a varied presentation style or to engage in monotonous presentations, and (7) keep the students' attention. These questions provided two answer choices, and so were coded as dummy variables. They were scored 1 if the professor remained stationary, lost eye contact, spoke extemporaneously, used a discussion format, created a casual climate, used a monotonous presentation style, and retained the students' attention; they were scored 0 otherwise. These measures provide some useful supplementary information to that obtained from the other measures.

Students' Evaluations

Students' responses to their professors' behaviors were assessed by a student questionnaire administered to the observed classes later in the academic term. The questionnaire, accompanied by computer-scorable answer forms, asked for basic demographic information such as gender, major, GPA, reason for taking the course, and previous experience with female instructors. The form also included five items from the student evaluation forms commonly used at the university, as well as six additional items designed to measure likability and to expand on the competence assessments obtained from the five original items (see appendix D). A fuller description and presentation of the questionnaire items, as well as of scale construction, are deferred to chapter 6, where students' reactions are discussed at length.

Analysis of Quantitative Data: Classroom Interaction

After constructing our measures from the observational and student survey data, we analyzed the data, looking for (1) gender differences in classroom behaviors and (2) the implications of these differences for students' evaluations.

Gender Differences in Classroom Behaviors

Our analysis of these differences consisted of mean comparisons; we used regression equations to test for significance. For each set of behaviors—basic instructional activities, authority management, and personalizing—our analysis considered the sex differences in these behaviors. To estimate the extent to which sex had independent, additive effects on the behaviors we observed, we estimated regression equations by sex of instructor (1 = female); the equations predicted the proportion of time for which these behaviors occurred in the classroom. We controlled for gender ratio of department (1 = male-dominated), the professor's rank (an ordinal measure), course level (an ordinal measure ranging from 1 to 9, with 1 designating 100-level or freshman courses), and the size of the class (estimated by the observer, and broken into six ordinal categories) because we wished to remove these possibly confounding influences from our analysis. No specific pattern of effects emerged for these

control variables; therefore, we do not discuss their effects. We estimated one equation for each measure of professors' and students'
classroom behavior.

As stated, we were concerned that these gender differences
would be more prevalent among faculty members in male-
dominated departments, but preliminary results showed no consistent pattern of differences. Although women in nonmale-dominated
departments were somewhat more likely to exhibit the most female-
typed strategies in the classroom, we found some important excep-
tions to these generalizations. Moreover, tests for interaction between instructor's sex and male domination of department on the
incidence of these behaviors were generally not significant. That is,
although the patterns generated by considering a four-way sex by
male domination of department difference were interesting, this
four-way difference was not statistically significant. The important
significant difference was still that between men and women, regardless of the sex ratio of their department. This finding also
helped to allay fears that the context of the courses in nonmale-
dominated departments might be more woman-centered, and therefore that differences in student responses might result from the
course context rather than from the instructor's teaching practices.
(Only three of the observed classes were gender studies courses.)

Students' Evaluations

To assess the implications of these behaviors on students' evaluations, we obtained a partial correlation between each measure of
classroom behavior and students' evaluations for men and for wom-
en students, controlling for many of the same confounding factors
discussed above.

We turn now to a discussion of our findings in the specific areas
examined.

Basic Instructional Activities in Academia

The faculty members we interviewed and observed used a diversity of strategies and techniques in the classroom. In general, university professors have a great deal of flexibility in performing the teaching aspect of their role. In most cases norms of academic freedom and personal autonomy preclude all but minimal interference. Certain activities, however, occur in most classrooms. These include carefully organizing lectures and other presentations so that they are easy to follow, soliciting students' feedback and checking the adequacy of explanations, and correcting any misinformation the students may have acquired. In the interest of promoting understanding and motivation among students, professors also encourage students' participation. This participation, sometimes taken for granted at the elementary and secondary levels, might be more difficult to achieve at the college level. Hence, the concerns and skills of women professors in facilitating interpersonal communication might be particularly valuable in helping them to manage the requirements of the professorial role.

We focus on two aspects of these activities: structured presentations and participatory learning. Both are common activities for university teachers (Centra 1987; McKeachie 1986). They are emphasized in teacher education as most effective (Rosenshine and Furst 1973) and are referred to as most appropriate (Duncan and Biddle 1974). Although there is no reason to assume that males and females will differ on the dimension of structured classroom presentations, women might be more likely than men to use participatory learning in their classrooms if they are more concerned with establishing interpersonal relationships and enhancing their students' sense of agency. Some recent evidence shows that women secondary teachers do, in fact, generate more student participation (Good et al. 1973; Brophy and Good 1974); Thorne suggests that this difference may carry over to the college level, in view of women's generally cooperative and symmetrical style of interaction (1979).

If women professors do make greater use of the participatory model, this difference would increase the amount of classroom time in which students are discussing the material, as we expected. We reasoned that learning in women's classrooms might focus primarily on the students as active participants rather than on the professor as the purveyor of knowledge.

Information Exchange as Good Teaching

Information exchange was the major goal in the classrooms we observed. Much of the classroom time was spent on lectures and presentations by the professor. A significant, though smaller, portion of time was given to interaction with the students. Although professors are not required to generate student involvement, some use of the participatory model is suggested for teachers in general (Duncan and Biddle 1974; Rosenshine and Furst 1973) and is counted among good teaching behaviors by university professors (Wotruba and Wright 1974). This approach presumably will increase the student's investment in the learning process. Because such investment is likely to facilitate the learning process, we expected some type of active participation by students to occur in most of the classrooms we observed.

We constructed specific measures to examine these behaviors. The two major dimensions of instruction specified above—structured presentations by the professor and participatory learning by the students—underlie the types of measures constructed. Structured presentations by the professor include two different sets of behaviors. The first set consists of managerial classroom behaviors such as giving assignments, making announcements, and going over the syllabus. These behaviors facilitate the learning process but are neither substantive (i.e., students will not be tested on them) nor evaluative. Second are the ordered substantive behaviors such as giving lectures, reviewing material covered, and emphasizing particular points. These behaviors are manifestly intended to convey knowledge; the students will be tested on this material.

Accordingly, we created two variables to measure the structured presentation dimension. We combined all managerial behaviors into a single variable called managerial behaviors. Such management of the classroom might affect how students learn the substantive material, as well as influence their judgments of a professor's competence and likability and the tenor of the class as a whole. Second, all behaviors that were subscripted as representing ordering, reviewing, or explicitly emphasizing certain substantive points were combined into a variable called ordered substantive presentations. In addition to these two variables, we constructed a combination measure of miscellaneous behaviors that occurred only infrequently: teacher's manipulation of artifacts (which makes presentation much clearer), unspoken behaviors (such as writing on the board, which also should clarify presentation), and professor's self-judgments of incorrectness (an indicator of the extent to which clarity of presentation is a valued goal). This latter measure summed all judgments of incorrectness subscripted as referring to self (see table 3.1).

The second dimension involves the quantity and the quality of professor/student interaction or the use of students' participatory learning. Generating students' involvement is a complex task, and doing so may overlap with the professor's structured presentations. For example, a professor could organize the classroom presentation in such a way as to facilitate feedback from students. The feedback might be used to check whether the professor is communicating with the class, but it also might be used as a way of involving students in their education. Recognizing the potential overlap, we decided to consider any input from the students as an indication that students' involvement was encouraged. Yet, because we also recognized the

TABLE 3.1

Proportion of Classroom Time Spent in Structuring Activities
(Observation Material)

Structured Presentations	Female Professors	Male Professors
Managerial behaviors	.039	.033
Presentation of material	.632	.704
Other/miscellaneous (correcting self, manipulating artifacts)	.001	.001

Note: No significant sex differences are found in any of these behaviors when sex ratio of department faculty, professor's rank, class size, and course level are controlled in regression format.

complexity involved, we distinguished among the levels of effort a professor expended to generate students' involvement. We divided behaviors into those which indicated minimal or mild use of participatory learning and those which indicated extensive use.

Mild efforts to involve students involve exchanges that require minimal feedback, such as the recitation of the "right" answer or a "yes" answer to a question such as "Do you understand?" Such behaviors in themselves suggest that professors are acquiescing in form to the principle of involving students but are not necessarily endorsing the spirit of this approach. The spirit is found in classrooms managed by professors who exert a stronger effort to involve students. In such classrooms, professors engage their students in exploring ideas about the material, in asking questions, and in sharing opinions. Through the use of humor, for example, they create classroom climates that are pleasant and warm. Their pedagogy may be experiential, such that students examine the artifacts being described, flip coins to "see" probability theory, or engage in sociodramas and mock debates. These behaviors—the encouragement of students' ideas and opinions and the use of humor and experiential teaching methods—we view as examples of strong efforts to involve students.

We constructed several measures to tap mild efforts to involve students. First, we considered the proportion of initiations by professors (presenting material) to be a negative indicator of use of the participatory model. Other measures seemed to be indirect indicators of limited use. They included proportion of time spent in professor's responses to students' questions, teacher's solicitations of clarifications ("What do you mean by that?"), and managerial solicitations ("Are there any questions?"). All three of these indicators involve the students only minimally in classroom interaction. They may serve simply to inform the professor of the students' comprehension rather than eliciting their active participation in initiating classroom discussion (see table 3.2).

Another subset of behaviors indicated extensive use of participatory learning. These behaviors, involving fuller student participation in the classroom, are a combination of all instances where students manipulated artifacts or engaged in other forms of experiential learning. We also created measures of teachers' general solicitations of students' input and of all student solicitations (questions or invitations to respond further). All of these behaviors indicated fuller student participation, in which students did more than take

TABLE 3.2

Proportion of Classroom Time Spent Encouraging and Permitting Students' Participation
(Observation Material)

	Women Professors	Men Professors
Mild Efforts to Involve Students		
Responding to questions	.083	.090
Soliciting clarification	.013	.012
Checking students' understanding	.024	.017[a]
Strong Efforts to Involve Students		
Soliciting students' input	.047	.029[a]
Soliciting responses from students	.051	.037[a]
Experiential presentations and activities	.023	.007[a]
Professors' and students' thought	.021	.007[a]
Professors' and students' laughter	.016	.013[a]
Participation by Students		
Total student input	.152	.096[a]
Students presenting material	.035	.013[a]
Students' solicitations of information	.017	.013[a]

[a]Significant sex differences occur at .05 level, controlling for sex ratio of department faculty, professor's rank, class size, and course level in regression format.

notes from lectures, ask for clarification, or respond to limited queries by the teacher (See table 3.2).

Several other measures served as indicators of the extent to which the classroom climate lent itself to a give-and-take between professor and students. We calculated total input by students as well as the proportion of time in which students presented material. We also measured the proportion of time given to professor's and students' laughter. These may be general indicators of the extent to which students' participation was encouraged; they certainly represent interaction patterns that may make the atmosphere more receptive to involvement by students (see table 3.2).

From several sets of data we gain multiple perspectives on these activities. The interview material allows us to explore the levels of commitment to good teaching held by male and female professors and to examine its meaning to them, including the salience of the teaching role, the professors' claimed commitment to structured presentations and to encouraging students' participation, their use of humor, and an additional concept related to the involvement of students, namely whether the classroom focus is on the professor or on the students.

The observational data permit us to examine sex differences in actual behaviors, including structured presentations, mild and strong efforts to involve students as participatory learners, and the actual amount of input by students.

Although our indicators of perceptions and attitudes regarding good teaching are not identical with the indicators of actual teaching behaviors, they emerge from the same theoretical perspectives. Hence, we will explore whether or not sex differences are consistent across the two sets of data.

Neither the status inconsistency/role conflict perspective nor the contextual/woman-centered perspective would lead us to propose that sex differences in overall basic instructional techniques would be great. Both males and females are socialized into an academic culture that values certain teaching activities; both males and females are in a situational context that demands at least an adherence to the goal of communicating knowledge in as clear a way as possible. If women are less secure in that context, as proposed by the status inconsistency/role conflict perspective, they are likely to compensate by thorough preparation and careful ordering of material, thus making their performance of this teaching behavior similar to that of their male colleagues. If they are not insecure in this context because they have already mastered the prerequisite skills (as attested by the attainment of the Ph.D.), as the contextual/woman-centered perspective would argue, they would still be similar to the male professors in the care given to organization of materials.

Although we do not expect the sex differences to be great, we propose that women professors will emphasize the importance of teaching more than men, will invest more effort in involving students, and will achieve higher levels of interaction with their students. Whether viewed from the status inconsistency/role conflict perspective or the contextual/woman-centered perspective, women are expected to be concerned more often with the well-being of others and to invest more in the establishment of relationships; these concerns are likely to carry over into the academic context and the teaching role. Thus, both perspectives predict similar outcomes concerning these behaviors.

The Salience of Teaching

The salience of teaching for university professors can vary a great deal. For some, teaching may be a highly salient role; for others it may be perfunctory and virtually ritualistic. For this reason we considered it necessary to examine the importance of teaching to the faculty; we did so through the interviews.

Being highly committed to teaching does not mean that one is an excellent teacher, nor is the reverse necessarily true. Even so, differences in the salience of the teaching role by sex may affect the amounts and kinds of satisfaction that males and females derive from teaching; in turn this satisfaction might affect their behavior.

Our interviews covered four issues that we used as indicators of the salience of the teaching role: (1) attitude toward teaching, (2) importance of being an excellent teacher, (3) amount of time spent discussing teaching, and (4) amount of time spent preparing for class. We assigned each respondent a score from 4 (high) to 0 (low) on each of the indicators; we summed these indicators into a single scale with a range of 16 (dedicated to teaching) to 0 (not invested in teaching). In addition, respondents volunteered information concerning the amount of life involvement they had in teaching, i.e., the relevance of teaching to their general state of well-being and to the management of their other role responsibilities. Each of the researchers responsible for the interviews independently rated from 0 (low) to 4 (high) each respondent's life involvement in teaching. The coders agreed on all but two judgments; those were negotiated. Life-

TABLE 3.3

Mean Scores for Salience of Teaching, Life Involvement, and Involvement
of Students, by Rank (Interview Material)

Rank	Salience of Teaching[a]		Life Involvement[b]		Involvement of Students[a]	
	Females	Males	Females	Males	Females	Males
Assistant	12.0	12.2	3.2	3.0	13.2	12.4
Associate	10.6	7.6	3.2	2.4	12.0	8.0
Full	5.4	4.4	1.4	.8	7.8	7.6
Overall mean	9.4	8.0	2.6	2.0	11.0	9.3

[a]Range possible: 0–16.

[b]Range possible: 0–4.

involvement judgment scores stand as secondary or confirmatory
data for the salience-of-teaching scores because there was considerable agreement between the two.

The mean salience-of-teaching scores and the mean life-
involvement scores by rank and by sex reveal no overall gender
differences (table 3.3). (To preserve confidentiality we do not present
the specific scores of individual faculty members.) There are, however, interactions between gender and rank. Specifically, commitment decreases as rank increases: male and female professors seem
to be equally dedicated; assistants are most dedicated and full professors least. The main gender difference occurs at the associate
level, where the women are more dedicated than the men; women
associates are closer to the assistant professors in their degree of
dedication, whereas male associates show midrange salience in
teaching scores.

The Life Course of the Teaching Role: Composites

Although we found no sex differences in overall salience of
teaching, we conjectured that teaching nevertheless might be salient for men and for women for different reasons. To explore this
possibility, we constructed separate composites of male and female
dedicated teachers based on the interview materials. These
composites—the male ideal-typic dedicated teacher and the female
ideal-typic dedicated teacher—do not represent any particular professor but depict a blending of characteristics found among the dedicated teachers.

The male ideal-typic dedicated professor sees teaching as "the most exciting, stimulating, varied profession that exists." He "loves it." He wants to do well at it. He spends nearly all of his time preparing, seeing students, and talking about teaching to his colleagues. A major portion of his preparation time and much of his conversation are devoted to "the mechanics of teaching," "designing teaching techniques," and sending memos to his colleagues about his ideas. Transferring content is not enough; "you must *find a way* to get the material into their heads." Teaching is a calling, a "mission much broader than the subject matter." Part of that mission is to find ways to teach his colleagues to teach better, to recognize students as human beings, and to devise techniques that work. When the techniques are successful, the professor feels good. When they flop, he designs new ones. He orders the remainder of his life around his teaching. This may mean that his wife "chooses" not to be employed or helps him with his curriculum planning and course presentation, that he "sacrifices" being an "ideal husband/father," or that in order to have any time to himself he "has to get out of town."

The female dedicated professor, as an ideal type, sees teaching as extremely valuable and important, perhaps "her most important professional contribution," "the thing [she does] which has the greatest value." She is "highly devoted" and "ego-involved." She "loves it." She spends a considerable amount of time preparing, thinking about it, counseling students, and talking about her teaching, especially with colleagues who are friends. For her, teaching means "communicating the subject matter *and* working with the students." Both are equally important. ("I get to read books I'm interested in and talk about them with others (students).") Students' responses are extremely important to her; she sees them as valid judges of her teaching excellence. She wants feedback, including negative feedback, so she can improve. If her class goes well, she shares her elation with colleague-friends; if it goes badly, "if the students become disenchanted—for whatever reason—everything else in (her) life feels out of whack"; doing a poor job makes her feel "depressed for hours—even into the evening." She knows she is a role model for her students, especially her female students, and strives to find ways to encourage them to succeed and at the same time to differentiate themselves from her—to find their own paths toward success.

The ideal-typic dedicated male professor and the ideal-typic dedicated female professor are similar in some ways. They both love teaching, want to be excellent at it, and expend a considerable amount of time preparing for it and talking about it. Both have high life involvement with teaching. Males, however, tend to be oriented more technically toward their teaching, and females more interpersonally. This difference can be seen in several ways. First, males discuss their dedication in terms of strategies and methods of teaching, whereas females focus on the content and on the students. Second, males talk to colleagues about those methods, whereas females tend to talk to colleague-friends about their feelings concerning a particular class or student. Third, male professors feel bad when a technique flops and rectify the situation by devising a different method. A bad teaching experience can be "turned around" by a new technique. On the other hand, female professors report feeling very bad and depressed when their classes go poorly. For them, rectification comes from obtaining students' input and evaluations. Fourth, dedicated males view teaching as a calling, a "mission." Their job is not only to teach students to enjoy learning—an abstract mission—but to teach other teachers—an external goal. Female professors do not report the same messianic zeal, but rather view themselves as individual role models who have a responsibility to create a more personal and more individualized relationship with their students.

Thus dedicated teaching seems to have different meanings for men and for women; the impact of dedicated teaching on their lives is different, both emotionally and structurally. Males tend to view the role as a "career" or a "cause" and to structure their private lives accordingly; wives and children accommodate to the demands of dedicated teaching. Female dedicated teachers apparently do not expect their families' lives to accommodate to the time demands resulting from their dedication. Unlike the males, however, they frequently mention the emotional consequences of dedicated teaching in terms of their feeling of well-being or depression. Dedicated males either do not experience these emotional consequences or erase them quickly by refocusing on teaching as a technical problem. Females focus on the relationship they develop with the students; males are more concerned with interactions with students, a precursor to involving the students in their learning. Thus, although teaching itself might not be much more important for women, the practice of participative teaching might have greater significance.

Almost directly opposite to those dedicated teachers are male and female professors—mostly at the full rank—who can be described as disinterested in teaching, not as devoted, dedicated, or involved. To what extent do male and female professors experience this noninvolvement in similar or dissimilar ways? To address this question, we constructed ideal-typic portraits of the male disinterested professor and the female disinterested professor.

The male disinterested professor sees teaching as "at best ancillary to the role of scholar/researcher," and at worst "the temptation of the devil," a waste of his talent and energy. Excellence in teaching is not a "priority" or a "primary motivation." He devotes little time to preparing for class, but he brings to teaching his "years of reading." Only occasionally does he discuss his teaching, and then with friends or spouse. He believes that students must motivate themselves; "spending time with such unformed and uninformed minds" is deadly to one's own development and growth.

The ideal-typic female disinterested professor views teaching at best as "what I do for a living," and at worst as "a chore, an interruption." Excellence in teaching is not important; in any case, "teaching takes up too much time." She rarely talks about it, and then primarily to a friend or spouse. Preparation time is minimal, but her "whole intellectual life is preparation." Students' feelings are not very interesting; their ideas, not very stimulating; and their evaluations, not very important. They are not her "constituency"; they are not the persons whose approval she seeks. She feels role-model pressures but believes that her life is her own and that she can act in ways judged appropriate by herself, not by her students. As these two ideal-typic constructions make clear, these men and women sound very similar; occasionally their language is nearly identical.

Disinterested professors spend a minimal amount of time preparing for and talking about teaching, have low ego involvement in being excellent teachers, and do not hold teaching as a priority. They have other interests. In the male professors' accounts, these other interests are specified as research and scholarship. That specification is not found in the women's accounts. We might view this finding as a continuation of the male *career* investment mode that was noted among the male dedicated teachers. That is, the male noninvested professors, although not concerned with teaching, make it clear that they are invested in the scholarship/research/writing aspects of the professorial role. The female professors do not specify the nature of their other commitments and interests. Further, although it is clear that teaching has lost its emotional salience for the noninvested women, the interviews give no sense that other aspects of their role have captured their emotional investment. Consequently we might hypothesize that as females move through the ranks, they become more like the males in the sense of abandoning the expressive dimension but are less likely to adopt the "career" and "mission" alternatives.

In summary, then, dedication to teaching is associated with gender and with rank. Dedication decreases as rank increases; the decrease is more rapid for men than for women. By looking at the ideal-typic male and female dedicated teachers, however, we find that the meanings of that dedication differ greatly by gender. Dedicated male professors are more technical or technique-focused in their orientation, whereas dedicated female professors are more relational or concerned with interpersonal relationships. Finally, the meaning of the teaching role for the disinterested professors is quite similar for both sexes; both men and women lack a personalized, affective orientation toward teaching.

Teaching as Structuring and Presenting

Behavior

Overall, men and women professors did not differ significantly in the importance they attached to the teaching role. Hence, we did not expect them to differ in their efforts to communicate the material clearly. In fact, both men and women spent a great proportion of their classroom time presenting material to their students. Even so, we noted great variety in how these presentations were handled. Some professors walked expansively around the classroom, making eye contact with virtually every student. Others stood quietly behind podiums, talking through a microphone to huge rooms full of students. Some were very dramatic; others were dry, crisp, and to the point. Some gender differences in style might have existed, but there were no gender differences in time spent presenting classroom material. Both sexes spent considerable time presenting material (see table 3.1); other related structuring activities took considerably less time. Men spent slightly more time presenting material, and women engaged somewhat more often in managerial (noncontent-related) activities, but these differences were not statistically significant when possibly confounding factors were controlled.[1]

Preferences for Structuring

The interviews contain more detailed information about professors' preferences for structuring classroom sessions. Although the structure and clarity of the material presented to the students are important features of teaching, our interviewees expressed preferences for different types of classroom structure. They differed in opinions regarding whether teachers should have a set agenda in mind for each classroom session. Here we discuss three types of structure: tight, loose, and "deceptive." As with the observation material, the use of these structures was not associated with gender or with rank.

Some of the professors described a style that involved careful preparation and tight organization. One male associate professor in the humanities explained, "You lecture as clearly and in as organized a fashion as you can." A woman full professor in home economics noted, "I outline, usually, or go with transparencies, but I get them organized. I don't like to be in a class myself where the teacher is fumbling around."

Other professors described a looser style that involved less preparation and granted more organizational responsibility to students. A male professor in the humanities said:

I make a practice of not reading [students' papers] that are going to be discussed in class ahead of time so I don't have preconceptions about them. Somebody in the class is going to be a critiquer so they read it aloud and start talking about it.

Similarly, a woman associate professor in home economics gave the following example:

I have a plan in mind but if students bring up some relevant subject matter we'll go with it because that's where they are. That's the teachable moment. That's the time to make use of that.

Other professors reported a style that was essentially a mixture of the tight and the loose. This style was described as one in which professors maintained an organized presentation of ideas while making it appear as if students controlled the classroom. That is, professors were able to orchestrate students' "spontaneous" presentation of ideas and insights to conform to their own plan for presenting information effectively; the class appeared deceptively loose. Two examples, one from a male and one from a female professor, are illustrative:

It's an easy, free-going class, though all the time I'm pulling the strings underneath. Someone describing me would say: "He's apparently very easy-going, deceptively loose," but underneath there's a very tight structure (male assistant, humanities).

There really is structure. I have in mind things that ought to be covered in a session but I let the students move in agendas of their own but try to get us back to what the agenda really is (female full, social sciences).

Although there were no gender differences in faculty members' reported use of any one of the three styles, we found an interesting difference in students' reactions, according to the professors' accounts. Women who described their style as loose and unstructured were more likely to report hostile reactions from students. As a woman assistant professor in home economics noted, "Some [students] get very upset if there is not a lot of structure." Several women felt that students saw a looser teaching style, when used by a woman, as indicative of incompetency. As one female associate professor in the humanities explained:

They think that I am too disorganized. I give the impression of not having things laid out in rigid structures. A lot of our students want coverage . . . I'm not a coverage person.

In summary, then, although all of the professors observed spent most of their classroom time presenting and structuring material, those whom we interviewed reported teaching styles that varied widely in degree of structure. The following orientations toward planning and organizing were evident in these descriptions: men were as likely as women to choose each of the styles, but women were more likely than men to report students' resentment of looser, less structured approaches. The data suggest that women's attempts to soften their presentations by loosening the class structure may incur resentment among students.

Students' Involvement

Structuring material is one aspect of teaching; generating students' involvement is another. Basically it is difficult to know whether students are absorbing material unless they provide a minimal amount of feedback. Waiting until examination time is both too late and too punitive a way to correct misunderstandings. Some instructors see their role as "teaching how to learn"; desiring more expanded involvement by students, they include them in a more complex array of activities.

Efforts to involve students can be seen in the observational data along two dimensions: mild and strong efforts. Mild efforts are activities designed to check students' understanding; strong efforts attempt to incorporate students more fully into the learning enterprise. Because we found no gender differences in the salience of teaching or in the structuring of material, we expected little difference in the mild efforts to involve students. Overall, these activities are simply an expansion of efforts to convey the material; the instructors are checking to make certain the material has been understood. We expected, however, to find gender differences in the strong efforts to involve students, given (nonfull professor) women's greater emphasis on the relationships they develop with their students, particularly on helping them to develop as learners.

Behavior and Perceptions

In observing these professors in their classrooms, we found few gender differences in what we call their "mild" efforts to involve students. These differences (table 3.2) are not statistically significant for the most part. Both sexes spent similar proportions of time answering and clarifying students' questions. These behaviors include asking, "By that do you mean. . . ?" "Where are you confused?" "I'm not sure I understand your question." Some students raised their hands to ask questions; others spoke out spontaneously. Some questions were posed as jokes that relieved the tension in a lengthy and technical explanation, others were asked seriously in quiet classrooms.

We noted gender differences, however, in one of these mild efforts, namely checking students' understanding. Women spent more time trying to determine whether students grasped the material. Women professors might ask directly whether the students understood or might devise quick methods for testing their understanding. They seemed to play a more active role in ensuring students' understanding, whereas men were more inclined to respond to students' questions once they had been asked.

More striking gender differences emerged when we looked at the professors' "strong" efforts to involve students. These activities include asking directly for students' input ("Does anyone know the answer to that question?" "Any thoughts about this?") and waiting to receive it, providing the opportunity for performing certain activities rather than simply talking about them (including the manipulation of artifacts), pausing for reflection or thought (by both student and professor), and laughing (usually together). All of these occurrences in the classroom suggest that more is going on than presentation of material; they indicate more interaction between student and professor. In the interviews, female professors echoed this concern with checking students' comprehension. Some professors felt that they were particularly sensitive to students who were confused but afraid to speak up, as in the following:

> I think I am extremely conscious of nonverbal cues and I don't think men are. Just out of all my experiences I can tell when a student is in distress and doesn't understand. I can tell when he or she wants to say something but isn't quite ready to raise the hand (associate, humanities).

In fact, women described more teaching techniques designed to determine when students were confused or misunderstood the material, and tended to let the correction of this situation guide their teaching. One woman, an associate professor in the natural sciences, explained:

> If the [student's] question indicates a lack of understanding of something that we have done previously or that has been in the [homework] problems—that the student has missed, generally then you do more than just interrupt [your lecture]. You may digress and rebuild because you don't want a stone out of place in mathematics.

As in the mild efforts, women might ask directly whether the students understood, or might devise quick methods for testing their understanding, as with applications ("Usually at the beginning of the class hour I will go over previous content and students will do the summary parts, which gives me an opportunity to see where they are."). These strategies were largely absent from the men professors' descriptions. Women seemed to be more active in ensuring that students understood, whereas men tended to respond to students' questions after they had been asked. Some of the activities were attempts to create a warm, pleasant atmosphere.

Other indicators show the outcomes of women professors' efforts to encourage students' participation: students had a significantly greater amount of total input in women's classes, presented significantly more material, and made a significantly greater number of solicitations than in male professors' classes. (See Table 3.2)

The interview material confirmed these findings. Many of the women professors described teaching styles that involved seeking students' input, using techniques such as asking questions, calling on students to define difficult terms, fostering group discussions, and requiring presentations by students as in the following:

> I find students' questions stimulating. The interrelation with students stimulates me. They make observations on points that I've missed or they ask me pertinent questions that I hadn't thought to ask (female, associate, humanities).

> I feel like I'm asking them to be not just rational and reasoning but also to feel things, be emotional. I expect them to not only think about the characters in the book but to feel about them, tell me who they hate and who they like. It's very important to me to respond that way to novels (female, assistant, humanities).

> In undergraduate courses I would say I carry the course on questions, ask a lot of questions. That I frequently stop and have the students work for me. The class is generally broken up between a much smaller segment of lecture—of my talking—(and) my response to difficulties that students are having with problems and some time generally for students to verbalize their own work—present it in some way (female, associate, natural sciences).

Not only did women professors describe a variety of methods to solicit students' input; they spoke more often about making genuine use of these contributions rather than merely giving students "time to talk." That is, they mentioned listening to what the students had to say and then incorporating this input into the classroom material. As one woman associate professor in English explained:

> The thing that students have always said about me in my evaluations is that I listen. And that very few professors do. They have a sense that I am really listening to what they say. I am conscious of that because I've worked at it.

In addition, women often said that they used experiential teaching methods in which they encouraged students to learn by doing and by experiencing the subject matter. They were more likely than men to list a number of such strategies when asked to do so (e.g., videotapes, case studies, interviewing a professional in the field, bringing in guest speakers for participatory small groups, creating performance art). Thus, in the women's but not the men's descriptions of their classes, time frequently was devoted to students' solicitations and students' presentations of material as an intentional pedagogical technique, as the following two women noted:

> I allow the discussion to take the direction the students essentially create, and go from there; at least when I'm at my best I do (female, associate, humanities).

> For an upper-division graduate course there would be a lot more lecture. I think I'm more inclined to interrupt my lecture with questions [for the students] than my colleagues are, and that my students are more inclined to interrupt me with questions. So that there would be, within the lecture, quite a bit of exchange between teacher and class (female, associate, natural sciences).

It is highly relevant to our argument that all but one of the strong attempts to involve students in the classroom occurred in women's classrooms significantly more often than in men's. Women strive more than men to create situations in which students are involved participants. The only classroom behavior that did not differ significantly was laughter, although even this occurred slightly more often in women's classrooms.

Humor. Our interviews provide additional insight with regard to laughter. Although we found no significant gender differences in the amount of laughter that occurred in classrooms, there were differences in the reasons men and women gave for the use of humor. As before, these gender differences seemed to interact with rank.

Male professors, especially assistants, used humor to "relax the class" and to encourage students' participation. Humor, by their accounts, helped informalize the class, as exemplified in the following statement by an assistant professor in the natural sciences:

> I'm lewd. I use semi-lewd humor because some of the things in the course relate to touchy sorts of things that need just a little humor to break the ice.

Men also used humor as "entertainment" to enliven their classes. They reported feeling good when their "jokes" were well received.

Female assistant professors rarely reported using humor purposefully in their classrooms, but tenured women frequently reported using it. Sometimes they used humor to deflect situations that were potentially a challenge to their authority, as the following two quotes illustrate:

[When students are rude], I just outsnide them in class (full, social science).

If they make a snide comment I try to keep it on a joking basis (associate, humanities).

The tenured women used humor for entertainment, as did the men. As one woman stated, "I use a lot of humor and funny illustrations . . . I put on a show." Some said it was an essential ingredient of teaching, as expressed in the following excerpt: "I don't think I've done a good job of teaching if we haven't laughed during a class period."

Thus, untenured males and tenured females are likely to claim humor as a strategy for good teaching. "Entertainment" is used by male assistants and by tenured women to create a friendlier and more pleasant atmosphere. Male assistants, however, are also likely to use it to "take the edge off" and to enhance students' participation, whereas tenured women use it to control inappropriate participation by students. In view of the options potentially available to women in situations where a student is "obnoxious" and "out of line" (such as directly confronting him or her, removing him or her from the classroom), women's use of humor suggests that they are trying to handle the situation in a way which disrupts only minimally the "open," "nonthreatening," "warm and personal" classroom environments they try to create.

Preferences for Involving Students

To assess the faculty members' preference for involving students, we used four kinds of information from the interviews: (1) stated use of an interactive class format, (2) desire for students' input in class, (3) desire for students' input in the form of evaluations by students, and (4) the professor's attitude toward students' opinions. We formed a single measure, commitment to involving students, by assigning each interviewed professor a score of 0 (low) to 4 (high) on each indicator and summing the scores for all four indicators. Hence, this measure, ranging from 0 to 16, reflects a professor's claimed commitment to involving students.

Nearly all faculty members claimed that they used an interactive classroom format such as lecture-discussion or question periods. Even the faculty in the natural sciences, where it is claimed sometimes that the interactive format is inappropriate, stated their preference for this approach.

Our respondents prefer the participatory model almost universally (table 3.3). In addition, there are no overall gender differences, although sex and rank interact. The lower the rank, the greater the claimed preference for involving students. As with the salience-of-teaching scores, female associates are closer in claimed preferences to assistants (both male and female), whereas male associates are closer in claimed preferences to full professors (both male and female).

Although male and female assistants score similarly, as do male and female full professors, we wanted to know whether the meaning of participatory education is the same for both sexes: do they have the same reasons for preferring it? To answer this question we drew upon the interview material both of faculty members who claimed strong preferences for involving students and of those who claimed little preference, and constructed ideal-typic portraits.

The male professors who are strongly committed to involving students discuss students' input as necessary and valuable because "we need to find what the students want to learn and what they expect" so we can "then do it." "Students won't learn unless motivated and interested." Further, because it is difficult to get students to discuss, sometimes it is necessary to "throw away a period just to induce them talking . . . and chattering about the material." Most of the interaction, however, takes place between student and professor.

The female professors who are committed to involving students, on the other hand, discuss students' input as desirable and valuable primarily because "through the interchange they (the students) develop a commitment to ideas"; "the process of learning is the learning." Eliciting discussion is not difficult because the professor creates a classroom atmosphere that is warm, relaxed, open, and nonthreatening. Best of all is the interaction that occurs between student and student, in which they "relate to each other, listen to each other."

Male professors who are strongly committed to involving students, then, see the interactive process as potentially a "time waste," difficult to sustain, primarily a relationship between professor and student, and valuable only to the extent that it enables them to find out what the students want to learn so they can teach it. On the other hand, female professors view the interaction as valuable in and of itself, and see themselves as creating non-threatening classroom atmospheres in which students can exchange ideas with each other, all for the purpose of increasing their learning capacity. Obviously these are very different attitudes toward the value of participatory education.

In contrast, males who are not strongly committed to involving students view students' input "as not a very useful thing" because "not everybody's opinion is equally good." They do "not even try to talk to the students" about their preferences and opinions regarding their education. Students are not able to evaluate because they lack basic competence.

Females who are not committed to involving students view students' evaluations primarily as judgments about the professor's personality rather than her competence. Students are "not particularly thoughtful" in those evaluations: "I know whether I'm prompt, prepared, or organized." These professors may not "even bother to read" the evaluations. They encourage classroom interaction, however, and will "*let* students move in agendas of their own (emphasis ours)" or will encourage questions to the professor, and they will "try not to talk down."

These less committed professors are fairly similar in their lack of respect for students' opinions of their teaching styles, but they differ in their classroom interaction patterns. Males tend to downplay such interaction almost entirely, whereas females adopt the model of students' interacting with the professor (rather than with other students) that prevailed among the younger men who strongly preferred student involvement.

Locus of Learning: Professor or Student?

Our analyses of the meanings of students' involvement and dedicated teaching for males and for females led us to an interesting conclusion; men and women professors seem to have very different attitudes towards students. Women professors, especially those who are dedicated to teaching and involving students, value students' contribution as an end in itself; for these women, stimulating students' interest and motivation is not simply a pedagogical technique. Dedicated female teachers see students as valuable sources of learning. Students' participation is a source of stimulation and learning for these women as well as for other students; affective relationships formed with students also are an important part of teaching. Even the women professors who do not prefer involvement by students encourage classroom interaction, albeit between student and professor.

Male professors do not mention the value of students as contributors, as collaborators, or as sources of knowledge or stimulation. Nor do they mention the importance of relationships that they form with students. Rather they see themselves as the *center* of the classroom, as the source of knowledge. Male dedicated teachers discuss the methods they might devise to convey the material more effectively; males who prefer students' involvement talk about the necessity of "permitting" students' participation in order to motivate the students or to find out what they know and what they want to learn. They do not regard students as having a genuinely active part in the learning process.

We term this stance toward students "locus of learning." Male professors tend to see the locus as almost entirely in themselves; female professors tend to see it as in the students. The gender difference is most visible in faculty members' assessments of "good" and "bad" classroom experiences, to which we now turn.

Professors' Best and Worst Classroom Experiences

In the interviews, we asked professors to describe a particular classroom experience that they felt was especially positive or rewarding and a classroom experience that they found especially negative or disappointing. Almost without exception, professors' descriptions of the best classes emphasized a high degree of involvement by students in the learning process (related to the blanket endorsement of students' involvement, as discussed above). This involvement was generated in a variety of situations, including interaction between students, interaction between a student and the professor with the rest of the class as audience, and periods during the professor's lecture when students listened attentively. Some professors described students' involvement in the context of a class discussion in which students became excited and "caught up" in relating their ideas and opinions: "Everybody was sort of leaping in saying things and getting involved and enthusiastic" (female, assistant). In other cases involvement occurred when some or all of the students were able to relate what they were learning to their personal lives: "We talked about heart attacks, and one student was crying because her father died of a heart attack, so it was a very emotional experience and the class all liked it" (male, assistant). In still other descriptions, involvement was fostered through simultaneous but independent intellectual discoveries in which students seemed suddenly to gain insight during a lecture: "It was one of those moments where the whole lecture section suddenly wakes up and you see that there is some comprehension" (male, associate).

In this sense the two sexes were highly similar, but the men and the women differed in one important way. Women were more likely to describe situations as most rewarding when students increased their independence from the professor, took charge of the progression of ideas, pursued topics outside the course requirements, or anticipated professors' major points. The following quotes provide examples:

[It happens] when a class starts to take over and I find that they're generating their own ideas and getting to the questions that I wanted to ask before I have to ask them, so that they move the discussion along (female, associate, humanities).

I'd gotten to the statement of the theory near the end of the class but I didn't have enough time to put the argument together. The next time we got back together they had constructed the argument. They were able to see exactly how this all fits together. That was exciting (female, assistant, natural sciences).

I could see them talking to each other, sharing ideas, relating to each other. They were not talking to me, they talked to me as if I were anyone else, a member of the class (female, assistant, social sciences)

On the other hand, men were more likely to describe their best classes as those in which they, as professors, had played a crucial part in generating students' involvement. In these descriptions, what made the class "best" was not only that students became highly involved in 'learning but also that the men felt satisfaction from being able to foster this kind of atmosphere. The following quotes are illustrative:

It was occasions when everyone would be talking, every one would be well read. It's like I motivated them to some extent. There was a good exchange of ideas based on the material presented so that when I walked in that room it was like I turned them on in some way or another (male, assistant, social sciences).

I had, in fact, covered the material well, conveyed the important facts and yet, in a sense, I entertained them and kept them interested in it. I had a little story to tell and it went over well and contributed to the atmosphere in the classroom (male, associate, social sciences).

There was a lecture I gave on the counter culture of the sixties that really struck home since I was a graduate student then and I used a lot of my own experiences. It really seemed to get things across to students . . . to the extent that they got up and applauded at the end of the lecture (male, assistant, humanities).

The professors' descriptions of their worst classes showed the same gender difference in perceptions of locus of learning. For the women, the worst classes were those in which the students' contribution to the classroom was lacking in some way ("They were completely disinterested"; "They had all been assigned to read a book and nobody had read it"; "I think the students were just all bad."). Among the men, however, descriptions of worst class experiences tended to focus on the teacher's deficiencies ("I skipped some material and had to go back and got confused"; "The most embarrassing ones are where you go in and actually get lost in your own explanation"; "When I use teaching techniques that just flop terribly.").

In sum, these findings constitute fairly strong evidence for gender differences in locus of learning. Males and females take different stances toward the students and have different perceptions of the student's role and competence in the classroom. Women professors tend to see students as more valuable contributors and as playing a more integral part in the learning process. Given this difference, we might predict more accurately the gender differences in students' involvement as observed in the classroom.

Students' Behaviors

Our observations permit us to say how much students actually participated in these classrooms. Although the total amount of student input is important in this regard, specific types of input might be more exact indicators of the "locus of learning" concept discussed above. In this situation students become a source of learning, along with the professor. Thus we give special attention to students' attempts to solicit information on their own from the instructor and to students' presentations of their own material or information. We expect all of these activities to occur more frequently in women's classrooms, particularly those in which the locus of learning is said to be with the student.

These gender differences do exist (see bottom panel of table 3.2). Students have significantly more input into women's classes. About one-sixth of the time in these classes, students are presenting material themselves (e.g., giving information from other sources or from class sources, short reports). They spend a smaller portion of that time soliciting information from the instructor.

Women, according to the interviews, are more likely to view their students as active, important contributors to the class. Our observational material confirms this point. Women are more likely to use techniques that increase the total amount of students' input into the classroom and to use teaching strategies that are student-centered rather than professor-centered. Although both males and females use similar teaching strategies, women's classes typically are different from men's classes in that students participate more and do so more independently.

Effect of Rank

As in the interview material, we found that the professor's rank affected these gender differences. We tested for this gender difference by estimating regression equations for all of the behaviors considered here that included a sex/rank interaction term. We found two significant interactions: those for presentation of information and for soliciting students' input. In both instances, gender differences were greater (and significant) for professors at ranks above assistant. Both assistant men and assistant women were quite likely to have involved students; tenured men were less likely to have done so. On the basis of the results from the interview data, this gender difference among tenured professors might be due largely to differences among associate professors (the majority of our tenured women). Women full professors might become more similar to men full professors in their divestiture of the teaching role; we cannot test this possibility with this sophisticated statistical technique, however, because there are not enough women full professors in the sample (or university) and because of the cross-sectional nature of our research design. Even so, tabular analysis shows that in keeping with the interviews, the women full professors we observed reduced their investment in teaching, particularly in participatory teaching.

Summary

These results show a marked gender difference in teaching styles. Although both sexes give the bulk of their time to structuring and presenting material, women professors are more likely than men to encourage students' input, particularly in ways that allow for a more independent student role. This difference is reflected in the behaviors we observed, as well as in the interview material dealing with attitudes toward students. Women professors view students as active collaborators in the learning process; hence, they give them more latitude in the classroom. These gender differences are especially true of associate professors; men assistants adopt the more female-typed participatory model, and female full professors divest themselves of this involvement.

Although these gender differences appeared, others did not. Women were not more committed to the teaching role nor to involving students. Both genders adopted normative stances typical of those in the teacher role, emphasizing the importance of teaching to approximately the same degree. Both were equally concerned with the clarity and structure of their presentations. Both believed that students' involvement was essential for successful teaching. The major difference was in their attitudes toward students, which conditioned the amount and the quality of student involvement that they encouraged and received. Women professors' tendency to make fuller use of students' input gives students greater latitude in the classroom, allowing them to contribute more substantively to the class. This possibility is related to the way in which authority is managed in the classroom, the topic of the following chapter.

Authority Management in the Classroom

Another way of looking at efforts to involve students is from the perspective of authority. Who has control of the classroom? Who is viewed as the expert on the subject matter—the students or the professor? The last chapter showed that women are much more likely to share this authority with their students, to encourage them as independent learners, and in the process to make students the locus of learning. Classes and seminars in which students take this role are the most satisfying to the women professors. Probably because they encourage it, women professors have more student involvement and activity in their classrooms. This aspect of their teaching—the relationships formed with students and the interaction within the classroom—is a great source of personal satisfaction for the women professors, as well as an important tool for communicating the material.

From the woman-centered/contextual perspective on gender differences, we would expect women professors to have worked out methods of wielding authority that were mutually satisfactory both to themselves and to the students. According to the role conflict/status inconsistency literature, however, women's attempts to manage authority in the classroom might lead to a chain of double binds; women are more likely to evoke responses in terms of their lesser status, female, than of their higher status, professor. Consequently they might not be viewed as legitimate holders of authority and thus could receive more challenges to their authority. On the other hand, if they adopt masculine sex-typed styles of interaction in an attempt to be viewed as legitimate, this strategy might lead to resentment and punishment by students (Kanter 1977). To attenuate these interactions, women professors might have to increase their feminine sex-typed behaviors. In doing so, however, they might be judged as incompetent (Eskilson and Wiley 1976; Meeker and Weitzel-O'Neill 1977) and, once again, not as legitimate holders of authority.

Therefore, according to the double-bind process, women face two primary authority issues: the *establishment* of their *legitimacy* as an authority and the *reduction* of their *appearance* as an authority. From our perspective, we would expect women to find successful ways of achieving these goals by using teaching strategies that establish their "power and authority" so that they could "abolish their power and authority" (Bridges and Wartman 1973, 78).

We consider several possible strategies that women can use simultaneously to legitimize and to reduce their authority in the classroom. These strategies center on encouraging participation by students. In addition to facilitating the teaching process, certain kinds of student participation also can soften the professor's position of authority in the classroom. To the extent that students are encouraged to make original contributions and, particularly, are encouraged or allowed to be assertive, they act as equal partners in the pursuit of substantive knowledge, reducing the focus on the professor as the sole authority. We expect women to engage in more of the behaviors that reduce their proprietary authority over substantive knowledge in the university classroom, as they have been found to do in secondary and elementary classrooms (Good et al. 1973; Griffen 1972). This finding strengthens our expectation that women professors will tend to use participatory strategies in the classroom.

To measure attempts to reduce the appearance of authority, we carry the notion of student participation a step beyond the basic instructional activities we observed in the last chapter. Students may participate in the classroom to increase their motivation and learning experiences. Beyond this point, however, they may be treated as fuller partners in the learning endeavor. The professor may yield some authority to the students; under such conditions they may engage in more assertive behaviors in the classroom. To measure this concept, we considered specific types of student input. We constructed several variables measuring students' assertiveness, including a measure of students' challenges, evaluative statements, and interruptions.

At the same time, women may use students' participation to legitimate their positions of authority. They may assert their right, as accorded by their professorial status, to set standards and to evaluate the correctness of students' comments. Thus, we expect that women professors, in an attempt to legitimize their authority as they reduce it, might give more evaluative feedback to students. We refer to this dimension of classroom authority as *evaluative authority*. Past work suggests that women teachers are more likely to exhibit behaviors reflecting such authority (Good et al. 1973; Lee and Wolinsky 1973).

Several of our measures showed attempts to establish legitimacy as an authority. One way in which professors establish control is by giving evaluative feedback—i.e., deciding whether a student's contribution is correct or incorrect. Thus, the basic measure of evaluative authority was a combination of positive feedback (personal and otherwise) and negative feedback (personal and otherwise). We also constructed a measure of unspoken positive feedback (head nodding and other behaviors—a summation of all positive feedback that was subscripted as unspoken).

Women are not free to use all types of authority-legitimizing techniques; in certain instances they might be more constrained than men. For instance, traditional notions of appropriate feminine behavior probably make it more difficult for women to use harsh or embarrassing control techniques, such as public humiliation, ridicule, or severe reprimands. Because such techniques contradict expected feminine behaviors, students might strongly resent (and sanction) women who apply them. Thus, to the extent that we find such techniques, we expect them to be more characteristic of men than of women.

We constructed a measure of the harshness of control techniques. To reduce the harshness of evaluative feedback, some professors qualify these judgments or convey them implicitly rather than directly. Hence, we distinguish between partial positive and negative feedback: partial positive feedback combines all implicit positive judgments and all partial positive judgments.

In addition, we use three direct measures of harshness of control: (1) the amount of ridicule used by professors, (2) admonishments, including severe disciplinary directives or threats to students as well as milder commands ("We will discuss this more later"), and (3) the extent to which professors interrupted their students' comments, a "harsh" interactive technique.

According to the earlier role conflict literature, men professors do not experience the same conflicts as women. Applying the interactionist perspective to the men's situations, however, reveals that they may experience the opposite problem: they may find that students are *too* accepting of their authority position so that they find it hard to encourage students to be active participants in the classroom. That is, students may be reserved in men's classes because of the role distance between them; this distance is based in part on the professor's established authority, which stems from the asymmetrical power and authority relationship between student and professor. Thus, men professors will not have the incentive to adopt authority-reduction strategies that characterize women. Their conflict, after all, is fundamentally different from that hypothesized to be experienced by women because it is a qualitatively different experience to operate from a position of legitimated authority—to have the authority and to choose to reduce it—than not to be granted that authority in the first place. The type of conflict is also different: the man is dissatisfied with the outcomes of role portrayal but is not pulled in two contradictory directions.

The structural role conflict/status inconsistency perspective would lead us to expect that women professors, more than men, will experience (1) challenges to their authority, (2) expectations that they will devise strategies to establish the legitimacy of their authority and simultaneously will reduce the appearance of authority, and (3) constraints on the types of authority-legitimizing techniques they use. Male professors, however, will recognize their legitimacy as authorities (though they find that it hampers students' responsiveness) and will be able to choose between strategies that vary in authoritativeness. If this is so, the work conditions of male and of female professors are qualitatively different.

The interactionist perspectives on gender differences offer a slightly different view of such tendencies on the part of women professors. Women may use less direct, confrontational, or harsh control techniques not only because they feel constrained by feminine gender role expectations and are attempting to reduce the hostility engendered by their authority position, but also because they regard harsh, confrontational approaches as less effective for both control and learning. If women do shift the locus of learning toward the student, the relationship serves as a potent mechanism for teaching in their classrooms. Thus they would be very hesitant to use control techniques that would disrupt that relationship. If the communication of material is their primary motivating principle, however, women professors would not shrink from giving corrective feedback to students, whether positive or negative. Thus, women professors might act to reduce their appearance of authority in the classroom, not so much to avoid sanctions by students as to promote learning.

Appearance of Authority

Professors' Perceptions

Our interview material lends some credence to the role conflict/status inconsistency arguments. Women professors perceived a need to establish their authority in the classroom, whereas men perceived a corresponding need to reduce theirs. As before, however, these differences were more true of assistant professors than of others.

Women assistant professors think their credibility is questionable in the eyes of their students. This perception is illustrated by the following statement of a woman in the natural sciences:

[I have] that attitude [which] is basically one of establishing myself as an authority figure. I have evolved this view of a professor as a person who is supposed to be really on top of a particular field . . . and not be wimpy about things.

This woman feels that students do not take her legitimate authority for granted. She has to convince them.

In contrast, male assistant professors recognize, as one male humanities professor commented, "People just automatically assume that a man has more authority immediately." As a male assistant professor in home economics stated, "I get from my students that they view men with Ph.D.s as brighter and more competent than women with Ph.D.s." Even when he was team teaching with women of higher rank, he said, "I would get all the questions. It's like I was in charge of the class."

At the associate level, women's doubts about the legitimacy of their authority as undergraduate teachers begin to moderate. For some women, however, graduate-level teaching may continue to pose problems, as this excerpt illustrates:

I do think the graduate students themselves expect a kind of authoritativeness that I don't give in the classroom. I don't feel comfortable with it and I think it has to do with my sex (humanities).

Once they attain full professorship, however, women no longer express any problem in establishing their legitimacy.

Difficulties with establishing legitimacy of authority apparently do not arise at any rank for male faculty members. One associate professor in the humanities said, "I *know* they (the students) see me as an authority figure." Males, however, state repeatedly that their authoritativeness has some negative consequences for their attempts to convey the material. At the assistant level the men are concerned that they might not meet students' "macho" expectations; indeed the professor might not want to meet them, but if he does not, the students will consider him ineffectual. (This concern parallels the assistant woman's concern that she not appear "wimpy.") At the associate level, the males seem less personally concerned about their image, clearer about how their male authority affects the students, and more likely to use that authority selectively and purposefully, as exemplified by the following:

> I want to partially maintain that (authority) but I also want to partially break that down so they will look for their own ideas. If I were a woman they wouldn't feel quite that authority (associate, humanities).

> I have to emphasize other roles [father, husband] to eliminate sex role stereotypes. But I teach with authority in a masculine way (associate, social sciences).

At the full professor rank the male either no longer cares about the issues or develops what might be described as a "yearning" or a "yen" for contact with students. Both a humanities professor and a natural sciences professor stated that they ask students to drop around to "just talk" . . . and that none do so. Here, then, gender differences in relating to students ultimately affect the personal satisfaction obtained from teaching.

Challenges by Students

Men and women professors perceived clearly that they differed in their need to establish themselves as authorities in the classroom, in terms of both classroom control and authority in subject matter. Even so, we did not observe gender differences in the challenges that women and men actually received from students in the classroom. The three relevant student behaviors we observed and recorded— challenges (arguing or questioning), evaluations (directly proclaiming something the professor says as right or wrong), and interruptions of the professor—occurred very seldom in any of the classrooms we observed[1] and were no more likely to occur for women

TABLE 4.1

Proportion of Classroom Time Occupied with Students' Challenges,
Evaluations, and Interruptions

	Women Professors	Men Professors
Challenges	.002	.003
Evaluations	.003	.002
Interruptions	.000[a]	.001

Note: No sex differences are significant at the .05 level, after controlling for
the sex domination of professor's departmental faculty, professor's rank,
class size, and course level in regression format (see text, chapter 2).

[a]Not actually zero; rounds to zero at third place.

professors. (See table 4.1.) Hence, men and women seemed to be
equally invulnerable to students' direct challenges to their authority. This observation is in keeping with the woman-centered/
contextual perspective on gender differences, in which members of
each sex are presumed capable of working out comfortable interaction patterns in their role relationships. This lack of difference
seemed to prevail despite the professors' perceptions that there were
differences and that students did challenge their authority. It should
be kept in mind, however, that we made our observations after the
academic term was well under way, so many challenges already
might have been met. In addition, these episodes are likely to be
relatively rare in the classroom. Perhaps more critical for our hypotheses and for the lives of the professors involved were the management techniques they were using.

Authority Management

In examining management techniques, we found gender differences both in perceptions and in behaviors. From both sets of data
we conclude that men and women professors display authority differently: women attempt to maintain the delicate balance involved
in establishing and reducing their appearance of authority simultaneously, while men seem to have more choices. For both sexes, but
especially for women, strategies often seem to be directed at maintaining an effective, perhaps nurturant relationship with the students while also remaining in charge.

Professors' Perceptions of Strategies

In the interview data, we looked at four commonly discussed classroom management problems. The first problem—
inattentiveness—was defined as behavior indicating students' lack
of interest, but not as disruptive to the classroom atmosphere (e.g.,
falling asleep or reading the newspaper). The second problem—
overt disruption—was defined as behavior that disturbed or inhib-
ited the presentation of students' or professors' ideas in class (e.g.,
talking during the lecture or monopolizing class discussion). The
third problem—challenging competence—was defined as verbal
statements made by students in class, attacking the professor's
knowledge and expertise. The fourth problem—lack of student
participation—was defined as students' unwillingness to interact
with the professor in the classroom context (e.g., lack of class discussion or lack of questions or comments). In each area, we determined
the degree of management problems that a professor experienced, as
well as the strategies used to resolve them.

We chose these problems not only because professors mentioned them frequently, but also because they represented four different situations in which professors could choose how to exercise
their authority. Inattentiveness, for example, could be ignored relatively easily because it did not bother other students. Thus professors had more discretion in deciding whether the situation war-
ranted intervention, as well as in choosing a response. In cases of
overt disruption professors were compelled to respond but could
vary the harshness of their reprimand. Challenges to competence
provided an additional element in that the professor's knowledge
and accuracy were questioned in public. Finally, lack of student
participation, like inattentiveness, was a nondisruptive problem
that allowed professors to decide whether and how to intervene. If
women are required to establish legitimacy while appearing non-
authoritarian, as argued by the role conflict/status inconsistency
perspective, and if men may choose between strategies that vary in
authoritativeness, this pattern should appear in professors' responses to these situations.

Inattentiveness. One common problem discussed by the professors concerned situations in which students were not paying attention: e.g., reading the newspaper, writing letters, falling asleep.
Reactions to this problem varied primarily by rank, although gender
differences in responses were apparent at some levels.

Women assistant professors claimed that they dealt with inattentiveness by ignoring it or approaching it indirectly. Those who ignored it did so because it did not disturb other students ("I figure that they are coming to college and they are paying for it, so if that's how they want to waste their time. . ."). An indirect approach was to involve the offending student in a class discussion, such as calling on him or her and asking for an opinion on the topic. The professor did this not to embarrass the student but to interest the student in the class.

Men assistant professors were likely to say that they took a direct approach by reprimanding the student in public or in private. Reprimands varied from explaining how inattentiveness would hurt their grade to confronting the students with the rudeness of their behavior, as in the following example:

> If a student is reading the school newspaper and not paying attention I will sometimes actually physically take the paper away and either demand an apology from the student or else tell him that attendance is not required, that it is an insult for him to be doing this (humanities).

At the associate level, reactions varied for both men and women professors. Some claimed to ignore inattentiveness ("I care but it doesn't disrupt the lecture") while others relayed disapproval by making eye contact with the student. Further, women at this level were as likely as men to reprimand the student directly. Even so, the nature of women's reprimands tended to be less harsh. One woman associate professor explained:

> I would just stop the student after class and *confess* to him that it is a bother to *me*, and that unless there is some overriding reason, I would *suggest* that if there is no way he can be attentive to the class, to not come (emphasis ours; natural sciences).

A different tone was apparent in male associates' comments as illustrated below:

> I tell them to take a little No-Doze before class. "Why do you give me your sleepy hours and give the damn bar your awake ones?" (humanities).

> They yawn. They read newspapers until you tell them not to. You say, "You are welcome to read the newspaper but not in my classroom" (natural sciences).

At the full professor level both men and women report little concern with inattentiveness. A few professors noted that they themselves had spent time as students writing letters or reading newspapers in class. Overall, however, the attitude among the senior faculty was that students, not professors, were responsible for maintaining interest in the classroom.

In summary, then, we found both gender and rank differences in the management of inattentiveness. Women assistants report ignoring the infractions or solving them indirectly by involving the student in the classroom discussion. Men assistants report reprimanding the students. At the associate level, although both males and females claim that they reprimand offending students, the approaches are qualitatively different. Whereas the women correct the student gently and privately for bothering them, the men are more harsh, direct, and public in their confrontations. At the full professor level, no gender differences appear because none of the professors viewed inattentiveness as a problem.

Disruptions. The second problem discussed by the professors involved situations in which students disrupted the classroom atmosphere. Disruption involved behavior such as talking with other students during a lecture, talking on the side during discussion, and monopolizing class time with constant questions or comments. There was no gender difference in the frequency of reporting this problem.

Talking during a lecture and side talking were approached directly by all assistant professors. Women were more likely to reprimand the students in an informal, offhand manner seemingly designed to reduce the students' feelings of embarrassment. The following is an example:

> The first few times I would do it jokingly and I might say it in terms like: "Shut up," "Shut up and get out," smiling. But if it happens often I might call them up after class and say: "Hey look, either cut it out or don't come" (humanities).

Male assistant professors were more likely to use public embarrassment as a negative sanction for talking. These men discussed how "making a big scene" in class was an effective way to stop the offending behavior as well as preventing future incidents by setting a clear example. As shown by statements such as, "It was very embarrassing for them" or "It was enough social embarrassment to stop it," these professors felt that embarrassing students was a legitimate way to confirm their authority in the classroom.

At the associate level, professors also dealt with the problem by reprimanding students. Women's reprimands stressed that they, as professors, were disturbed by the behavior. One woman explained:

> I can't stand idle conversation in a large lecture, and I have stopped a lecture and explained to them that I must require that they be involved in what we are doing (natural sciences).

Another woman related an incident in which she required two students to sit apart during classes to prevent further disturbances to her teaching. The men associate professors' reprimands emphasized that the talking was disruptive to the other students in the class. They made statements such as, "It's difficult for other people," "It's causing us a problem if there is a second conversation going on," and "You are probably disturbing other students." This strategy is interesting in view of the finding described in the last chapter, which showed that men tended to focus on themselves as the center of classroom learning. In this case, the men focus more on the students being disturbed by disruption while the women's accounts emphasize disruption as troubling to them.

At the level of full professor, disruptive talking was addressed directly in class by a simple statement asking the student to "stop or leave." Absent from these reprimands were justifications for delivering them (e.g., "You are bothering me," "You are bothering other students"), as in the following examples:

> I told the person in class that if he wants to come to class he shouldn't carry on private conversations (male, humanities).

> [I say] if you want to talk to each other go out in the hall and talk. You are welcome to leave any time you want (female, social sciences).

In addition, full professors seemed to encounter this problem less frequently than associate and assistant professors.

Disruptions of the classroom atmosphere, according to the professors, also occurred when one student monopolized teacher-student interaction. As one man explained, "Sometimes you get a student who has to answer every question" (associate, social sciences). All the professors, regardless of gender or rank, handled this problem in a similar manner. They spoke privately to the student, asking him or her to save questions or comments until after class. Further, the professors reported not being wholly satisfied with their eventual resolution of the problem. The following example is typical:

> I had this one guy that myself and the TAs nicknamed "The Pest." The problem was that usually his questions did not pertain to what we were dealing with that day or that week or whatever. I don't think I handled it very well because I let him continue with it for about two weeks. And by the end of the two weeks whenever he raised his hand the rest of the class just groaned audibly. Finally, I took him aside at the end of two weeks and asked him when he had questions, would he think about them a little more. And if he thought that they were still important questions to please come in during my office hours (male, associate, humanities).

In summary, handling of disruptions generally differed by rank and sex. Female assistant professors reprimanded students in a friendly, conciliatory way, whereas male assistant professors embarrassed the disrupter in public. The associate women discussed the disruption with the student as personally problematic for themselves, whereas male associates told the offender that he or she was bothering the other students. Only at the full professor level is there a convergence: both males and females publicly stopped the disrupting student(s) and did not, apparently, soft-pedal or justify their responses to disruptive behavior. There were no differences, however, in how professors handled the classroom monopolizer. They discussed the issue with the student after class once the problem had become habitual and entrenched.

Challenges to competence. The third management problem involved dealing with students who verbally challenged a professor's competence. Responses to this situation revealed some interesting gender and rank-related differences.

Challenges seldom were reported by women assistant professors; the few who mentioned them interpreted them positively. One woman explained, "I guess I'd like to see more of that. To me it says that they are thinking, they are moving, they are questioning" (home economics). Another woman stated, "To me, the best thing that could happen in a class would be for them to disagree entirely with me and open the book and try to prove to me that I'm wrong" (humanities). Two assistant-level women, however, mentioned non-verbal behaviors that they interpreted as challenges. One explained, "The men in my class, some of them start with very negative attitudes and sit in class with this smug look on their face, very skeptical" (humanities). Another gave the following example: "Every once in a while you get what I call a 'smirker,' somebody who just sits in the back of the room and has this wide smirking expression on his face. I've had women, but more often men, doing this" (natural sciences). Both women handled this problem by ignoring it, and in most cases the student eventually stopped.

Men at the assistant level mentioned encountering verbal challenges more frequently. Their response was to divert the challenge to another time and place, usually later in their office. The following is an example:

I had one student, very bright, very nice fellow. But he kept attacking me for being anti-Soviet. I said, "OK. That's fair if you want to attack me from that point of view. Why don't you read this? Come in and we'll discuss it and see what happens" (history).

At the associate level both women and men reported verbal challenges from students. Women tended to handle them in class with a considerable amount of patience, even when they that felt the student was wrong, as in the following two examples:

I thought that this course would never get off the ground. I dialogued with him every day, not all period, but once every day for three weeks. During the third week he finally began to realize what I was trying to say. It was a hassle (social sciences).

Once in a while you get sort of a smart aleck. Usually, if you give them enough rope, they'll hang themselves. The rest of the class will start laughing at them (humanities).

On the other hand, men associate professors were more likely to handle challenges not by discussing them but by explaining how the student was wrong or inaccurate. Usually they responded to the challenge with a defense of their own position:

He challenged things like the dates. I said, "I know they are the dates because I just put this lecture together." He said, "No, you're wrong." I said, "Well, I don't think I'm wrong." It went on like this so I finally said, "Look, I know I'm right . . . if you'd like to come to my office, I'll show you books and articles that I used to draw up my lectures" (humanities).

Full professors encountered verbal challenges less frequently, but women mentioned a few instances. In these cases the challenges came during the first few days of classes and were met directly and immediately. One woman, who teaches a course about science, reported that she always receives a few challenges at the beginning from male science majors. Another woman in science reported that she met initial resistance until she demonstrated her knowledge of the subject matter. Both women characterized these instances as minor testing behaviors that they dealt with routinely and quickly.

Thus, challenges to competence were not experienced negatively as long as they were direct; even though junior women were annoyed by the indirect challenges, they handled them by ignoring them. Associate women used class time to discuss the challenges with the students; full professors stopped the direct challenges quickly and ignored indirect challenges.

Male professors at the assistant and associate ranks, but not at the full rank, reported challenges to their competence. Assistant males diverted the challengers and asked them to come to their office later to discuss their differences. Associates, on the other hand, told the student in class why his or her ideas were inadequate or wrong.

Lack of student participation. The fourth management problem concerns the extent to which professorial authority interferes with encouraging student participation. Often students were reluctant or unwilling to participate in classroom professor/student interaction; sometimes they failed to take part in classroom discussions or refused to ask questions or make comments concerning the course material. Because all of the professors wanted to use at least some of these types of interaction in their teaching, the potential for such problematic behavior was present for all our interviewees. Our analysis revealed differences related to gender and rank.

At the assistant professor level none of the women reported problems with eliciting student interaction in the classroom. In fact, several felt that the fact that they were female encouraged input from students. As one woman explained, "I really do think that one of the reasons students are more open to asking questions . . . [is] because I'm a woman" (social sciences). Another commented:

I'm very concerned about how my students are feeling, how they're reacting with each other and me. I think that's very much because women are taught to think about it and worry about it and men aren't as much (humanities).

As noted previously, men assistant professors tended to describe the opposite situation. They felt that their status as males hindered professor/student interaction, and they mentioned several strategies designed to de-emphasize their authoritativeness. These strategies included joking with the students ("I use a little humor to break the ice"), using relaxed body language ("To promote class discussion . . . my usual style is to sit on top of the desk cross-legged or lotus position or legs hanging"), and dressing informally ("I don't wear coats and ties"). Some of the men articulated the conflict they felt between expectations that they be authoritative and that they be open to students' spontaneous ideas and questions. A social science professor described this situation as "an anomaly for males": they are expected to behave authoritatively and still be responsive to students "rather than just saying, 'Well, here it is. Take it or leave it.'"

At the associate level, women professors were unanimous in their enthusiasm for an interactive classroom teaching style. Some used it exclusively; others combined it with lecturing. Absent from these women's comments were mentions of specific techniques used to "break the ice" or problems in inducing students to talk in class. In addition, all the women mentioned that they enjoyed the give and take of classroom interaction.

Men associate professors also elicited interaction with students, but a different attitude was apparent. The men were more likely to view class discussions and students' comments as something they *should* encourage rather than as something they enjoyed and *wanted* to encourage. In the words of one professor:

In an honors course of fifteen students you get lots of feedback, and in a course of 200 students you may have to point a finger, but I do it. It's worth *wasting* ten minutes out of an hour lecture to get feedback from the students (emphasis ours; natural sciences).

In addition, associate males, like the assistant males, felt that their position as an authority constrained student-professor interaction. These associate professors mentioned various ways in which they managed this situation. One humanities professor, who felt that his students were frightened of him, tried to counter this problem by dressing informally and allowing students a great deal of time to make their comments. Another in the social sciences explained:

> I try to get to class early and try to talk with different students before class begins, just to be there [to] introduce elements of informal exchange.

At the level of full professor, few difficulties with eliciting interaction were mentioned. Two of the women said that they experienced this problem only when students were unprepared; most of the men did not mention this issue. Two of the men, however, noted that it had become harder for them to relate to students, although they tried to do so. One man explained:

> When I came here as a young instructor I had a much easier rapport with students. Then I found as I became an associate and a full professor, was on university senate, was a publishing scholar, there was a gap created by my status (natural sciences).

In summary, females regardless of rank reported no problem in involving students in discussion. Assistant and associate male professors believed that their status as males and as authority figures had a dampening effect on classroom interactions; some full male professors saw *themselves* as having difficulty relating to the students. These data support our contention that both male and female professors view students' perceptions of appropriate gender role behaviors as an important influence on students' degree of comfort interacting with university faculty members. Women faculty felt that their gender encouraged students to participate in the education process; men viewed their gender as a hindrance to student-professor relationships. This finding is consistent with predictions based on the status inconsistency and role conflict literature.

Rank and gender were related to faculty members' responses to management problems. At the assistant and associate levels, females reported using strategies (ignoring, gently reprimanding, encouraging discussion of professor-student differences) that legitimated their authority even as they reduced their appearance of authority. These strategies made it more likely that a positive rapport between student and professor would continue to exist. In contrast, the male assistants and associates stated that they reprimanded publicly and harshly, corrected students' misconceptions directly, and "point-proved" outside the classroom. That is, the males reported less hesitancy in displaying their legitimacy as authorities; they used strategies that were more direct and more potentially humiliating to the students. Men in authority management situations seemed little concerned with future implications for their relationships with students. In a related vein, men reported having more difficulty in inducing students to participate or in relating to them. Although they used their authority to maintain control in classroom management situations, it seemed to have a dampening effect on students. Thus, the role conflict/status inconsistency arguments seem to account for these differences more accurately, though the woman-centered/contextual arguments help us to understand why some female faculty members were better able than others to manage their classroom authority.

Classroom Observations

In the interviews, the women described themselves as using less harsh techniques to establish their authority. Within these constraints, however, they seemed quite determined to establish that authority. On the other hand, the men were concerned that they had too much authority and spoke of strategies that they used to reduce their appearance of authority—though simultaneously, perhaps unwittingly, they used harsh control techniques that widened the gulf between student and professor.

We observed some of these trends in the classroom. One set of indicators used in our observations concerned subject matter authority—that is, the professor's perogative to judge students' contributions as correct or incorrect. Because women professors received more input from students and seemed more concerned than men with establishing their subject matter authority, we expected that they would engage in more of these judgments. The results are especially striking with respect to positive feedback: women spend twice as much time (on average) as men in making positive judgments about students' contributions (table 4.2). We also expected women to engage in more unspoken encouragement (such as head

TABLE 4.2

Proportion of Classroom Time Spent in Giving Corrective Feedback
(Evaluative Authority)

	Women Professors	Men Professors
Positive evaluations	.033	.016[a]
Negative evaluations	.007	.005[a]
Unspoken positive reinforcement	.000[b]	.000[b]

[a]Sex differences are significant at .05 level, controlling for male domination of professor's departmental faculty, professor's rank, class size, and course level in regression format.

[b]Not actually zero; rounds to zero at third place.

nodding) but found so little of this behavior for either gender that it was virtually nonexistent (less than .1 percent of total classroom time for either sex).

Whereas women professors understandably might use certain authority management techniques more often than men, they might use other types less often. We expected women to use harsh or direct techniques less often and to use modified or indirect techniques more often (as indicated in the interviews).

Because of their hesitancy to use male-typed techniques and their concern with relating to students, women might give evaluative feedback in a less direct way; hence, we expected them to use more partial positive ("yes . . . but") and partial negative feedback ("no . . . but") than the men. Admonishments that include routine directive statements ("Open your books," "Turn to page 31," "Notice the underlying point here"), as well as harsher statements, along with other authority control strategies, might be less characteristic of women. We predicted that ridicule, which includes only harsh statements ("That's a *dumb* thing to say!"), would be used less frequently by women. Finally, because interrupting other speakers is a dominance strategy that women are unlikely to use in other settings (Thorne 1979; West and Zimmerman 1983), we expected women to be less likely to interrupt students here as well.

Women give more partial positive and negative feedback than do men, though the gender difference for partial negative feedback is not statistically significant (table 4.3). Neither difference is as great as the gender differences in unqualified positive and negative feedback (table 4.2). Hence, women show no strong tendency to qualify their evaluative feedback, probably because this feedback is a

TABLE 4.3

Proportion of Classroom Time Spent in Giving Harsh or Modified
Corrective Feedback

	Women Professors	Men Professors
Modified		
Partial positive evaluations	.005	.002[a]
Partial negative evaluations	.002	.001
Harsh/Direct		
Admonishments	.004	.002[a]
Ridicule	.000[b]	.001[a]
Professor interrupting student	.002	.001

[a]Sex differences are significant at .05 level, controlling for sex domination of professor's departmental faculty, professor's rank, class size, and course level in regression format.

[b]Not actually zero; rounds to zero at third place.

major source of their classroom authority. It also might be a way to encourage participation by students. Women are simply more likely to give positive feedback of *any* kind—direct or modified. Perhaps their "yes. . . but"s are simply indirect (and softened) ways of giving negative feedback to students.

Harsher control techniques occur with less frequency. No gender differences exist in the tendency to interrupt, though (unexpectedly) women use admonishments more often and (as predicted) use ridicule less often. Women's greater use of admonishments makes some sense because of the extent to which our admonishment measure is confounded with evaluative control and managerial behaviors; both types of behaviors are more characteristic of women. The gender difference in ridicule suggests that women indeed refrain from using harsh control techniques; this finding coincides with the female professors' own accounts of using gentler, less direct strategies in dealing with management problems.

Rank Differences

To learn whether tenure differences had discernible behavioral consequences, we reestimated the regression equations, adding an interaction term for sex and tenure. Few of these interactions were significant; thus, we do not present the results but simply describe those which were significant.

As with good teaching behaviors, the greatest gender differences were found between the tenured men and the tenured women. Tenured women were more likely to use behaviors that increased their evaluative authority (specifically, positive and negative feedback) and decreased their subject-matter authority (specifically, students asking questions and volunteering new ideas). These effects occurred independent of course level and class size. Also independent of course level and class size, male and female untenured professors tended to be quite similar in their use of authority: junior faculty members of both sexes were likely to increase evaluative authority and to reduce subject-matter authority.

Unfortunately, our observational material cannot be compared directly to the major rank differences we discovered in the interviews because our observations include few women at the full professor rank (reflecting their extreme underrepresentation in the university). As the reader will recall, however, assistant women, assistant men, and associate women are similar to each other in management strategies, and the tenured women in our observational sample are primarily associates; therefore, the strong sex differences between tenured males and tenured females are consistent with the interview findings. Males and females at the lower ranks are similar in style. At the associate level, males begin to be less invested in teaching interactively and less concerned with management strategies, but women retain that investment until they attain full professorship. At that point they are similar to their male full professor counterparts; neither sex is much concerned about authority issues.

Summary

These results show important gender differences in the management of classroom authority. Although both sets of data suggest few gender differences in the challenges that professors actually receive in the classroom, marked differences exist in *perceptions* of challenges to authority and in strategies for managing them. The differences are interesting, especially when related to differences in basic instructional behaviors. The men themselves make the connection between their authority position and their ability to involve students in the classroom. They may not realize, however, that their authority management strategies may deter students' involvement. Whatever their awareness, this lack of involvement clearly troubles them. The men, then, use their authority at the cost of involvement by students.

The women's position is the opposite. They share authority and receive students' input, but not without cost. The women (especially untenured professors) struggle to assert their authority position. To handle this situation, the women in our interview sample, especially assistant professors, acted to establish the legitimacy of their authority position; they felt that students had more doubts about their competence than about that of male professors. Even so, their strategies for establishing legitimacy seemed designed to avoid students' resentment. The women used less direct, less harsh, less punitive means of dealing with students than male professors, and granted considerably more subject-matter authority to their students. Women were, however, quite firm in their stands on authority; they made full use of their evaluative authority, and as their rank increased, they reported themselves to be quite adept at confronting direct challenges by students. As they approached the end of their careers, they seemed to derive more satisfaction from their teaching than did the men.

Although the double binds hypothesized by the role conflict/status inconsistency literature do seem to exist for women, particularly in their perceptions, they were not nearly as pronounced as one might expect. In fact, women seemed to establish and maintain their authority in the classroom with relative ease, being careful not to disrupt their relationships with students in the process. This finding provides support for the contextual/woman-centered approach, which predicts that women's greater repertoire of interpersonal techniques and skills allow them to manage conflict situations effectively. This possibility will become clearer in chapter 6 when we consider students' reactions to the professors we studied. Meanwhile, we turn to personalizations, the final category of teaching behaviors that we considered.

Personalizations: Look Into My Life

Thus far we have found the women professors more likely than the men to use teaching strategies that enhance their relationships with students. Although this propensity seems to decrease with rank, the woman professor in general is much less self-focused than her male counterpart and more concerned (and more successful) with involving students in the learning process, nurturing these relationships, and maintaining control and establishing authority in a way that leaves her relationships with the students intact. On the basis of the contextual/woman-centered arguments presented in chapter 2, we expected these tendencies to appear.

Considerable research supports the proposition that women are more concerned with making connections than with establishing autonomy (Belenky et al. 1986; Gilligan 1982; Rubin 1983). Women play important expressive roles in groups (Meeker and Weitzel-O'Neill 1977) and more often choose person-oriented as opposed to task-oriented occupations (Rossi 1968). The use of these behaviors, however, might be the result not only of personal choice but also of expectations held by others; the use of personalizing might even conflict with the teaching styles that women would prefer to use in certain situations. For example, Wikler's study (1973) of the incoming 1973 students at the University of California-Santa Cruz (UCSC) found that students expected women professors to be more "approachable" than their male counterparts. Similarly, Wikler's study of female UCSC faculty members (1976) revealed numerous ways in which women professors were "propelled" into personalized teaching styles by both students and colleagues. Female faculty respondents described students who expected their female professors to act as "sounding boards" for their "great ideas" (1976, p. 10), those who expected "mom and dad" treatment from male and female faculty teaching teams, and female students who looked for personal and intellectual nurturance from women faculty members viewed as role models.

Personalizing behaviors are not only more comfortable for women and/or in greater demand by students and colleagues. In addition, these behaviors might serve the same function as the authority reduction techniques: they might "cool out" students' resentment of women in authoritative, prestigious positions. Hence, they may be essential to the woman's attempts to establish herself in the classroom, as well as being personally preferable or expected. Thus, they also would be predicted by the role conflict/status inconsistency perspective.

From this perspective, personalizing would do even more than the authority reduction techniques discussed in chapter 4 to reduce students' resentment of female professors. Personalizing is consistent with traditional female role expectations, and it broadens the scope of the teacher-student relationship. Because female professors might be somewhat reluctant or uneasy about wielding their authority, and, more important, because they might be more concerned than men about maintaining their connections to students, they might be more likely to personalize than men.

As with authority reduction techniques, however, the willingness to personalize might represent more than an attempt to reduce students' resentment; women might see personalization as a way to foster the relationship as a vital mechanism for learning. Women professors, for example, might be more likely to believe that students learn by applying the material to their own lives and that they are more likely to feel involved in the classroom if the professor knows them by name.

Our data permit us to look at professors' ideas about personalizing inside and outside the classroom. Personalizing, as we have conceptualized it, refers to professors' attempts to create or preserve the personal, caring, human elements in their interactions and relationships with students. In classroom situations, it is true, professors can personalize by using examples from their own and students' private lives. Yet they can go further; they also can focus on the students' experiences, acknowledge their contributions and empathize verbally with their struggles and successes in mastering the material. Any of these behaviors will help to create a more humanistic, more person-oriented learning atmosphere. Outside the classroom, professors can chat informally with their students, consult directly with them during office hours, and listen to their personal concerns and problems. In the interviews, professors discussed their perceptions of the amount of personalizing in which they and their students engaged, the content of the personalizing, the setting for personalizing (inside or outside class), and their attitudes toward it. From our observations we can gauge the actual incidence of personalizing behaviors on the part of both professors and students in the classroom. These include personal acknowledgments of students' contributions (e.g., "Thank you, Ben"), empathizing with students ("I know that was a tough question"), personal statements about the self and about the students, and personal statements from students about their own lives.

We constructed several variables. First we created a general personalization variable that summed professors' references to the students' personal lives or to their own. Then we created separate variables measuring professors' references to self and to students, as well as all personalizations by students. These variables showed the extent to which the classroom environment permitted or encouraged the sharing of private experiences.

We included two further measures of the extent to which professors created personal classroom atmospheres: acknowledgments of students' contributions (which might include thanking the student, referring back to the student's idea, or using the student's name); and a measure of the professor's empathizing with the students, involving statements such as "I understand this is hard for you." These behaviors seem to be directed at enhancing the personal, intimate quality of classroom interaction. They involve professors and students in interactions based on needs for respect and intimacy, and they permit more personal contact than we might expect typically to find in the classroom.

Personalizing in the Classroom

Self-Revelations by Professors

Classrooms can provide an opportunity for professors to share their personal histories and experiences with students. In the interviews, many of the professors reported that they revealed personal information about themselves, their families, and their careers to students. Fewer male professors than female, however, reported using this type of personalization. We also found an important difference between men and women regarding the content of the information shared and their attitudes toward sharing: men gave "less personal" personal information. One assistant professor in the humanities characterized the information he gave students as "the nonpersonal-type personal information." Other men said that they talked primarily about their academic career and professional qualifications and often did so only on the first day of class. "Where I'm from, what degrees I have, what my interests are in the scholarly sense" were the topics discussed by one man in the social sciences.

Whereas many of the men regarded relating personal information as a duty and as a presentation of credentials, the women professors preferred to convey personal information by drawing on their private lives as well as on their careers for examples and illustrations. One woman full professor related, "I think I probably talk more than men about things in my life. I talk about my children and I will tend to use them for examples." A woman associate explained, "I talk about my experiences. They know me as a person fairly well." Frequently, however, the women chose examples and illustrations that they viewed as relevant to the *students'* lives.

When women professors discussed their careers, they tended to do so in order to defend their subject-matter authority rather than in an attempt to personalize, as revealed by the following statements of two female professors:

> I can see them looking at me and thinking, "Oh yeah, sure." Well then I'll stop and tell them some of the kinds of things that I've done, and I haven't always been here teaching (home economics).

> I get (challenges) in the big classes very early in the course, particularly from science majors who are, I suspect, willing . . . to challenge my science background. But it's very easily set off. I tell them about my education background (humanities).

Overall, then, women were more likely than men to report presenting personal information to their classes and to view these personalizations as "building bridges" between the students' experiences and their own. Women reported using their private lives and families as examples throughout the course. Only when challenged did they present detailed career information and qualifications; these challenges, incidentally, occurred at all the ranks. On the other hand, when men personalized, they tended to describe giving information about their own careers and credentials in a semiformalized presentation.

Our observational material confirms the interview findings. Gender differences were revealed in the professors' personalizations.[1] (See top portion of table 5.1.) Overall, women spent more of their classroom time making personal statements, either about their own lives (family, experiences, training) or about the students' lives (e.g., "You know how it is when you live in a dorm. . ."). As the interviews suggest, women do not spend more time talking about themselves; it is probably the nature, not the incidence, of these comments that varies by sex. Men talk about less personal career aspects of themselves; women talk about more personal family and feeling aspects of themselves. Our observation coding scheme did not distinguish between types of personalization in this way, but we did observe a marked difference in the tendency to personalize in ways pretaining to the students' lives. Again, women seem more intent on making this connection, drawing students in, and making the learning environment relevant and comfortable for them. Yet this emphasis on connection has an ulterior motive: it serves the teaching function. As one interviewee said, women tried to "reach students where they live . . . as a way of understanding" class material.

Professors have several other behavioral strategies they use to make the classroom more humanistic and more person-centered, and to reduce the role distance between students and faculty. These

TABLE 5.1

Proportion of Time Spent in Personalizing in the Classroom
(Observation Material)

	Women	Men
Personalizations by Professors	.026	.015[a]
Related to self	.015	.011
Related to students	.011	.004[a]
Expression of empathy for students	.001	.002
Acknowledgment of students' contributions	.017	.012[a]
Personalizations by students	.011	.000[a,b]

[a]Sex differences are significant at the .05 level, controlling for professor's rank, male domination of professor's department, class size, and course level in regression format.

[b]Not actually zero; rounds to zero at third place.

behaviors include empathizing with students through such verbal statements as "I know you've been trying hard to keep up with all of this reading" (i.e., verbal indicators that the professor is taking the student's point of view) and acknowledging students' contributions by personal communication (e.g., calling a student by name) or expressions of gratitude (e.g., "Thank you for your insight," "As Josh has reminded us. . ."). Expressions of empathy were given rarely by either sex and, so, were no more typical of women than of men. Most of the verbal empathizing that did occur involved discussions of course requirements—the difficulty of the material, the "fairness" of an examination question, or the scheduling of tests. These discussions are no more likely for men or for women, especially if women are more likely to set out very specific class requirements (as indicated by our unreported interview material). Women professors, however, were more likely to acknowledge their students' contributions. They called them by name more often, thanked them for comments or insights, and referred back to their contributions later in the class. These strategies served both to reinforce their relationships with students and to draw students into the learning process.

Self-Revelations by Students

Another opportunity for personalization in the classroom arose when students shared their private lives and experiences with each other and with the professor. We also saw this tendency in both the interview and observation data. In the interviews, one woman in the humanities explained, "I want it to be a kind of personal experience so I don't mind if they talk about themselves." A man in the natural sciences who relied on students for nutritional histories stated, "There's the obvious jock in the class, and he is more than willing to tell them what he has to do to maintain his weight, his schedule, what he eats and why, etc." In several of the professors' descriptions of their "best classes," students exchanged personal information with each other and with the professor. Overall, however, there were no systematic differences in sex or rank between professors who reported personalization by students in the classroom and those who did not. The type of comments made by students, however, differed with the professor's sex.

The observations, in fact, revealed striking gender differences in this regard. Students did more personalizing (e.g., made statements about their families and experiences) in women's classes than in men's (table 5.1). The women generally were more likely to use strategies to reduce the role distance between themselves and their students by increasing the student-centeredness of their classrooms. The strategies most often employed by women were using material relevant to the students' personal lives and encouraging the students to discuss their experiences in the classroom. Female professors made the classroom experience personally relevant to their students. In contrast, many of the personal statements made by male professors referred to themselves. On the basis of the interview material, these statements might have involved their own careers and credentials rather than any personal self-revelations. Thus, female professors made more attempts to personalize their classrooms; their students apparently responded by engaging in a greater amount of personalization than in men's classes.

Differences by tenure. As with the other behaviors we have discussed, we were concerned that the observed gender differences might be especially strong for assistant professors, who because of their nontenured status might experience more status insecurity than other professors. Women assistant professors might be especially likely to use personalizing strategies to enhance their relationship with students. Men assistant professors also might adopt these strategies because of their concern with engaging students. As men came to feel less need to draw students in, they might drop these strategies from their repertoires (as might women, though later in their professional lives).

To test these possibilities, we reestimated the regression equations that gave us the significant results reported in table 5.1, adding a sex-by-tenure interaction term. We found significant interaction for three behaviors: personal statements related to students, personal statements related to self only, and acknowledgments.

Untenured women are significantly less likely to personalize than their higher-ranked counterparts. Untenured men, on the other hand, are more likely to personalize than their tenured male colleagues. These results may be explained as the result of status anxiety, although in a way more complex than we initially thought. Untenured women might feel more insecure in their roles as professors and might keep a lid on the extent to which they personalize in the classroom. Interview material (not reported here), for example, shows that female professors believed they had to "sit on" certain aspects of their "femininity" to prove themselves competent, and that they lifted those personality constraints only after they had secured tenure. Once tenured, they stated that they felt more able to reintegrate their "personhood," to stop being "this asexual creature."

That is, tenured women, freed of intense status anxiety, simply might be more able than nontenured women to follow their own preferences for establishing student-centered teaching climates.

On the other hand, if the interview materials are correct, the greater personalizing behavior of the assistant males probably emphasizes their career accomplishments. Bringing credentials to class might be a technique that they use to increase their sense of worth and to decrease their status anxiety; they are not necessarily trying to increase the human-centeredness of their classrooms. In addition, as we saw in the preceding chapter, this behavior might represent the men's attempts to overcome students' hesitancy to participate in the classroom. Once tenured, these men (like their tenured female colleagues) might feel freer to return to personal preferences, thereby reducing the amount of behavior that seems to indicate attempts to humanize the classroom. The interview material contains some evidence that male full professors in particular were disenchanted with students and with teaching, and placed higher priority on their research.

Personalizing Outside the Classroom

Situations outside the classroom also provide opportunities for informal interaction between students and faculty. In the interviews, professors talked about three kinds of extraclass personalization: chatting, listening to personal problems, and negotiating grades with students.

Chatting

Chatting involved an exchange between student and professor of largely nonacademic, somewhat personal, usually superficial information (e.g., student's future plans, other courses taught by the professor). Although we have classified chatting as an out-of-class form of interaction, it was sometimes described as occurring before or after class or during the midclass break. Other chatting contexts mentioned by faculty were in a professor's office, on the campus grounds, and in situations created by chance meetings (e.g., in the supermarket). Men more often described chatting in the classroom, while women more often reported this form of interaction outside the classroom proper, as in these examples:

Now I go over earlier and try to get to know some people in the front row. I try to chat with them (male, full, humanities).

In this course we have coffee every day for ten minutes and we discuss a few things as well (male, associate, natural sciences).

[On campus] students will just come up . . . and start talking to me about things, about the subject matter and sometimes about their lives (female, assistant, social sciences).

They just show up, and they want to talk about research, or they want a reference, or they are interested in such and such. (female, full, humanities).

In summary, although both men and women professors chatted with students, men described this type of informal conversation in the classroom while women described more examples outside the classroom. For women, extra-class chatting might indicate greater willingness to be personally interested in students because such chatting is not constrained by the bell or by the formal setting of the classroom. The professor and the student can interact in a less limited way. Perhaps students also chat with faculty members for different reasons, bringing more personal conversations to the woman professor's office hours and more public exchanges to their male professors within the confines of the classroom. In addition, as discussed in chapter 4, men reported that they used chatting to reduce their appearance of authority, whereas women did not.

Counseling

Personalization also occurred when students discussed their personal problems and difficulties with professors. They were most likely to do so during the faculty member's office hours. The content of these conversations was characterized as more serious than that of chatting. One assistant male professor related the following extreme example:

She would come in and tell me all the latest adventures at home. Her parents got a divorce; her brother declared he was a homosexual; her sister ran away; the dog died; her father was on the verge of losing his job, on and on (natural sciences).

A woman professor stated, "All the students that have ever had nervous breakdowns in this place have had them in my office" (associate, humanities).

Although both men and women reported that their students came to them with personal problems, the men were more likely to view this behavior as an annoyance, and several questioned the motives. One professor thought the students were trying to make "brownie points." Another pointed out, "I think you come to a teacher with a *sob story* for either a legitimate or illegitimate reason" (emphasis ours). Many reported trying to discourage students from relating personal problems, as in the following examples:

> I say, "I have to do some other things," which is not a lie. If they're not talking about something of real substance that relates to the course . . . I'll just say, "I have other things to do, and you'll have to excuse me" (male, full, humanities).

> If they begin to talk about personal problems, I tell them that I am not trained to deal with those kinds of problems, I'm not comfortable dealing with that . . . I make it clear in the course outline that . . . I won't do it" (male, associate, social sciences).

On the other hand, the women professors' attitude was that they should listen when students brought up their personal problems, even if this behavior was time-consuming or occasionally inappropriate. Women were likely to point out that students' academic performance could be affected by their personal lives and that students deserved to be heard before they decided whether or not a problem was a legitimate topic for discussion. One woman related the following story in full:

> Last quarter I made it very clear to the students that a quiz or a test missed was a zero. There were no makeups. [One student] was giving this course everything and missed one of the midterms. It turned out that her sister's boyfriend had attacked her mother and she had called the emergency squad; the police came, just like something from a soap opera. But those things happen in the lives of our students, and it makes quite a difference in how they perform academically. I don't know how you can say you won't listen to those things (associate, natural sciences).

The women professors, however, did not report becoming highly involved in their students' personal problems. Many stated clearly that they did not counsel more seriously disturbed students. In the words of one woman professor, "I have developed a policy. I listen to find out the extent of the problem and what role I could play in it" (associate, humanities). Another commented, "Sometimes I can't give them any advice and sometimes I can" (full, home economics).

Both men and women professors, then, regardless of rank or department, reported that students discussed personal problems in their offices. Men were more likely to be suspicious of this behavior and reported strategies that they used to avoid this situation. Women, however, tended to view listening to personal problems as a teacher's responsibility because these problems could affect academic performance. Even so, they maintained a personal distance from the problems and, if necessary, referred the student to a professional counselor.

Male and female professors had differing perspectives on personalizing in general. Women were more likely than men to cite examples from their own lives in the classroom, to listen to students' personal problems outside the classroom, and to chat with them informally in situations and contexts removed from the classroom.

From these results it would seem that women have managed any potential role strain between being a woman—friendly and nurturant—and being a professor—distant and authoritative—by reducing the professional distance in the classroom itself, in their offices, and in unscheduled informal interactions with students. Men, on the other hand, see themselves as personalizing in the classroom by talking about their academic careers and chatting about course work and students' career plans, but they avoid the greater personalizing inherent in revealing personal information about themselves or in listening to their students' personal problems.

Negotiating Grades

A third and final situation involving personalization by professors occurred when students came to their office hours to discuss grades and to negotiate arrangements such as grade changes, making up missed work, or extra-credit assignments. The content of these interactions was characterized as more serious than either chatting or counseling because often the student's scholarship or academic status was at stake. Both men and women professors reported that students came to them to protest a grade and/or to ask that it be changed. Men were slightly more likely to characterize grade change negotiations as commonplace; many of the women claimed that this had happened to them only "once or twice."

One reason for the foregoing difference might be that the female professors described a series of "bolstering strategies," techniques they used to draw the line about what was negotiable and to maintain that line. These included placing elaborate statements about grading criteria on their syllabi, appealing to strict university regulations forbidding grade changing, assigning a paper early in the term to provide students with feedback while it was still possible to drop the course, backing up a graded student project with lists of comments and reasons for the grade, and discussing their grading philosophy in class. All of these bolstering strategies were designed to avoid confrontations with students about grades; one female mathematics associate professor limited students to written protests and refused to engage in any face-to-face discussion about why she had given a grade.

The male professors were more "negotiation-oriented" in their approach to requests for grade changes. They more often described sitting down with a student and going over an examination or an essay to point out where the students had lost points or had failed to develop an idea. In other words, the men focused on demonstration and negotiation in resolving students' objections to evaluation. They also were more willing than the women to make actual alterations in grades. That is, the men more often reported situations in which a review of their grades showed where they had erred in assigning the original grade. One male assistant, who taught primarily large biology lecture sections, described his response as follows:

> If they are really close to a cutoff, we then contact their TA. We say, "Do they merit the benefit of a doubt, maybe, to pull them over the hump?" We recheck to make sure the grades are reported accurately and added accurately.

Another male associate history professor gave this explanation:

> First what you do (is) you check the numbers. Have you made a mistake with the numbers? It happens, and you apologize profusely for being so dumb. If it's something else, like an examination . . . you go through it with them. Occasionally you'll realize that you did not understand what they were saying. They were right. And then you change the grade. More commonly they won't have understood what you'd been trying to say, and hopefully they leave satisfied with the grade you gave them.

A full professor in education described his strategy:

> In both cases I gave students an opportunity to express and to
> indicate what their concern was and why they felt that a grade
> change ought to take place. . . . I changed one but not the other
> because I didn't think it [the student's rationale] was a legiti-
> mate argument.

These patterns are interesting because they seem to suggest
that men place greater reliance than women on their positions as
authorities in dealing face-to-face with students who demand re-
dress. In contrast, female professors' tendency to chose strategies
that avoid confrontation might suggest that they are less comfortable using their authority directly. We might have predicted the
opposite if, given the women-centered argument, we had assumed
that women's greater interpersonal facility would make them more
comfortable in dealing directly with students in these matters. One
possible reason why women sometimes prefer to avoid office-hour
confrontations might be that students are more threatening to their
female than to their male teachers when disputes arise. To investi-
gate this possibility we asked all the professors to describe any
situations in which students had tried to manipulate them with
threats of abuse or suggestions of intimacy in exchange for special
treatment.

When queried, the men at all levels and in all disciplines believed that a few female students were willing to exchange sex for a
grade; some professors were able to relate incidents in which they
felt they had been propositioned. One sociology professor described
times when female students' "statements and posture seem to be
suggesting the possibility of sexual conduct." A man in history felt
that the behavior was more flirtatious than serious ("they try being
cute and little-girlish"). These stories were paralleled by the accounts of some women who reported male students who had tried to
charm them into higher grades or easier assignments.

Moreover, both sexes reported incidents in which students had
threatened or bullied them over a grade; in a few cases the situations became quite serious and involved lawsuits or the need for
security protection. Although these incidents were more frightening
to the women than to the men, female professors did not appear to
be more subject to such manipulations than their male counterparts.

In sum, although female faculty members were more willing
than men to use their office-hour interactions to listen to students'
personal problems, apparently they drew the line at entertaining
direct challenges to their authority over grades. Men, on the other
hand, were more willing to demonstrate their authority to students
and to show them where they were wrong during office-hour confer-
ences; they avoided students who wanted to discuss more personal
issues. Finally, both sexes described instances of seductive or threatening behavior by students, apparently a somewhat common experience for faculty members at this large state university.

Summary

These findings demonstrate that men and women professors
are quite different in their attempts to personalize their classroom
atmospheres. Neither sex showed a greater tendency toward self-
revelation in the classroom, though our interview data suggest that
the content of women's revelations might have been more personal.
The greatest gender difference concerned women's attempts to relate to their students' personal situations. In our interview data,
female professors reported more of these attempts; our observational data *show* women making more of these attempts. Female professors more often used examples relevant to the students' personal
lives and encouraged students to relate their own experiences to the
class. In essence, they seemed to focus more on the student as a total
person, incorporating students' experiences into classroom presentations, listening to students' problems in their offices, and chatting
with students outside the classroom.
    Although these behaviors simply might make the situation
more comfortable for women because of prior sex-role conditioning,
they could serve another pragmatic function. The women believed
that they enhanced the students' learning potential by making the
students the focus of learning. From the woman-centered/
contextual perspective, such a strategy shows the strengths of wom-
en's responses to a particular situation. From a role conflict/status
inconsistency perspective, we could argue that personalizations enable women to establish their authority in the classroom without
violating sex-appropriate behavioral norms. Along these lines, the
women professors adopted a more formalized, less interactive position only when grades were at issue, while the men engaged in
direct interaction and authority with students who came to their
offices. For whatever reason, personalizing behaviors appear to be

especially important to women professors; men, on the other hand, are less likely to use these methods and might in the end, be less satisfied with the relationships they form with students as a result. In the previous chapter, we showed that the men were unhappy with this outcome because they wished to reduce the distance between themselves and students.

Professors' concern with their students' feelings about them may influence their perception of role conflict in the professorial role. Accordingly we turn now to the question of how students react to the differences we have discussed in basic instructional techniques, authority management, and personalizations, as measured by students' evaluations.

Students' Reactions: Evaluating
Men and Women Faculty

Our purpose is not only to document the relationship between gender and teaching styles in the university but also to explore the implications of these styles for the men and women who use them. Students' reactions are especially critical because they might help us to judge the relative efficacy of the woman-centered/contextual perspective as opposed to the role conflict/status inconsistency perspective. In many instances the women professors believed that others had conflicting expectations that they be both feminine and competent and complained about the resulting strain. Many of their classroom behaviors could be viewed as strategies to manage that strain. Certainly the perception of competing expectations for women professors is significant in its own right, as it increases job demands faced by women. Equally important, however, is the question of whether students do, in fact, hold these conflicting expectations or whether they judge men's and women's different teaching approaches as equally competent. By looking at students' evaluations we can begin to address the complexities of this issue. If students react negatively to the women's approach, this situation could be problematic for several reasons.

Students are the primary recipients of instructional activity, and so become important role partners of professors. The interactionist argument discussed earlier asserts that behavioral resolutions of role conflicts are guided by the expectations and reactions of significant others. For exponents of this view, the immediate social environment is a crucial determining factor. In the case of professors' classroom situations, students constitute an important group of significant others. How students treat a professor, especially in the early years of college teaching, has an important impact on his or her professional identity (Wikler 1976). Students' evaluations of faculty performance, moreover, often affect career advancement in promotion and tenure decisions (Centra 1987; Martin 1984; McKeachie, 1987; Unger and Jacobson 1978). Therefore, we expected professors' teaching strategies to be determined in part by students' evaluations, which we conceptualize as varying along two major dimensions: competence and likability.

According to symbolic interactionism (cf. Stryker 1980), a process of negotiation occurs between the partners of any role relationship. This negotiation is directed toward achieving common understandings of the situation; it enables the partners to act in concert and reduces much of the frustration that potentially exists in any relationship of mutual dependency. If professors disagree with students' behavior, problems arise and negotiations must follow. The more powerful role partner (here, the professor) has the ability to influence the interaction process more profoundly.

Acknowledged less often, though emphasized by symbolic interactionism, is the idea that the less powerful role partners also have this ability. Particularly in a classroom setting, where students greatly outnumber the professor, the students' definition of the situation must be taken into account. According to our theoretical perspective, each role partner adjusts to cues from the other about expected role behaviors throughout the semester. The professor may give cues ranging from the subtle (gently guiding the mode of questioning) to the dramatic (failing a student on an examination). Students also may use the same range of cues, from the subtle (asking questions hesitantly after class) to the dramatic (challenging the professor's accuracy during class). As the professor and the student send out and receive cues, they tend toward "alignment" (Weinstein and Deutschberger 1963). In most situations, role partners achieve higher degrees of mutual understanding and mutuality through time. Failure to do so results in tension and discomfort in the role relationship.

The likelihood of continuing tension is high when role partners approach their relationship with deep-seated expectations arising from "master role" statuses that might supersede the temporary expectations of the immediate role relationship. Gender roles are among the most powerful and most pervasive of these master roles. They operate in all aspects of our lives, and their expectations are always present. To the extent that gender role expectations conflict with those for the professorial role, members of the gender in question will find it difficult to function satisfactorily (as far as students are concerned) in the role of professor. Because students typically have some input into the process of evaluating their professors, they become especially powerful role partners. If women are systematically judged less effective, their chances for promotion and tenure may be jeopardized.

There is substantial evidence that students make judgments about both the competence and the likability of their professors (Elmore and Lapointe, 1975; Kaschack 1978; Martin 1984; Wikler 1976), and that these ratings have a certain consistency and validity across time and place (Lamberth and Kosteski 1981; Marsh 1984). Although the feedback effect might not be immediate (Kulik and Kulik 1974), the evidence suggests that certain characteristics of teachers considered here, such as the use of humor (Check 1979; Perry, Abrams, and Leventhal 1979) and gender (Aleamoni and Thomas 1980; Basow and Silberg 1985), affect students' evaluations. Characteristics of the students themselves also affect their judgments of professors (Aleamoni and Thomas 1980; Follman 1975); in many instances students reward professors for engaging in behaviors that students like or enjoy, especially when students' reactions are assessed with very general measures (Aleamoni and Thomas 1980).

We have postulated that the teaching strategies considered in this study will appeal to students' evaluative criteria for both competence and likability. We expect the use of basic instructional techniques to be related positively to judgments of competence, although they also might affect evaluations of likability. Students, for example, might interpret structured presentations, the checking of students' comprehension, and the attempt to generate students' participation as indicating general concern for students and for their progress in learning the material; such a perception would create an impression of affability as well as competence on the part of the teacher.

Authority control (legitimizing) techniques also are expected to increase competence ratings, although harsh control techniques are expected to reduce likability ratings, particularly for women. In several studies, college students were found to judge female authority figures who behaved punitively more harshly than they judged punitive male authority figures (Martin 1984; Unger and Jacobson 1978). Authority reduction techniques and personalizations probably enhance the professors' likability. Yet in line with the double bind hypothesis derived from structural role theory, use of these techniques might lower the professors' competence ratings (Martin 1984; Wikler 1976). Recall the literature (discussed earlier), which suggests that women are perceived as less competent because they are less assertive, less directive, less controlling, and more focused on interpersonal relationships (Eskilson and Wiley 1976; Meeker and Weitzel-O'Neill 1977; Thorne 1979).

According to both the interactionist and the contextual/woman centered views, another scenario is possible: if differences in teaching style do exist, students might well appreciate the styles used both by men and by women (Babladelis 1973). Males and females, using different approaches, might achieve similar goals effectively. In fact, it is possible that women would be perceived as more effective teachers, though the literature does not lead us to expect this outcome. Possibly, students, coming to classes with notions about expected male and female behaviors, reinforce or reward members of each gender for meeting those expectations. This possibility is particularly likely for personalizing behaviors; at least one study has found that students have a strong desire to contribute personal material to their classes, a behavior that has been found to make (male) professors feel uncomfortable (Adler 1984). If women professors do more personalizing, particularly in encouraging the contribution of personal material from their students, students might react with respect and appreciation. Certainly, many educational specialists currently advocate the widespread adoption of this approach. As Martin states, "Valuing rationality for its contributions to self-control and personal autonomy . . . embraces [an] ideal that cuts the self off from others" (1984, p. 7). She adds that we must seek ways of promoting "generative" love in our teaching process, involving the "3 C's . . . care, connection, concern" (1986, p. 9).

If this is the case, women might be rewarded by students (rather than sanctioned negatively) for departing from the male-identified professorial role expectations. Thus, the professor who is warm, nurturant, and egalitarian with her students may find that she is judged to be as effective or, perhaps, a better professor than her male counterparts. This interactionist view does not perceive the woman as confronted by two rigidly opposing role expectations. One and possibly both sets of expectations can be modified through the negotiation process between or among role partners.

Once again, however, in view of the assumption of wide variability among women professors (which would be predicted by the woman-centered perspective), it is also likely that some women will not conform to whatever expectations students hold for female faculty members. That is, the woman professor whose personality departs from what is considered feminine might find that students expect her to be more relationship-centered and more personal than she cares to be. Finally, perhaps female professors are more adept at displaying a wide range of teaching behaviors, which allow them to match their teaching style to the particular demands of students in certain classes. In this case the woman is viewed as somewhat of a performer, using her wide repertoire of interaction skills as needed. We could hypothesize that students, already unsure of what to expect from a professor with discrepant statuses, will tolerate a broader range of attitudes and behaviors from their female teachers and possibly will give a more positive evaluation to women faculty members who display them. All of these possibilities are considered next. We obtained students' reactions through a time-honored mechanism: the student evaluation.

Professors' Views of Students' Evaluations

In considering the professors' views, we first explored the issue of evaluation. We asked our interview sample to describe their feelings about students' evaluations, particularly whether these evaluations led to improved teaching or affected the professor's own chances of promotion and tenure.

Formal evaluation by students, encouraged officially and strongly by this university administration, was conceptually interesting for a number of reasons. First, such evaluations by definition elicit students' perceptions of what constitutes adequate or good teaching. Second, as we shall see, the evaluation process tends to depend heavily on how students judge a professor's personality (as well as competence) and ability to treat students fairly (as well as to exercise authority and control). Thus, the topic of student evaluation led our interviewees to consider how many of the issues explored in earlier chapters intersect in students' reactions to their classroom and office-hour experiences.

Every one of the professors offered an opinion about the validity of students' evaluations and about the criteria that the evaluators were "really" employing. Moreover, all of our interviewees claimed that they collected evaluations from students as a regular practice in all their classes. Many of the professors used the standardized multi-item evaluation forms (SETs) developed by the university; others used an additional or alternative form developed by themselves or by their departments or colleges. Male and female professors were equally likely to have developed their own unique (usually open-ended, essay-style) evaluation format, and they were equally likely to use the multiple-choice, computer-scored SET forms provided by the university. Overall, then, there was little divergence in the likelihood or manner of eliciting students' opinions of teachers' performance.

A common theme in professors' discussions of the evaluation process was that students were not qualified to judge a professor's knowledge of the subject matter or the appropriateness of topics covered in a particular course. Many agreed, however, that students were competent to assess other aspects such as whether or not the professor was organized and prepared, whether he or she talked too fast or too softly, and whether a book or article was boring or interesting. As one male associate in history explained:

> Students can't be and they really aren't the final judge of what is necessarily always good in teaching. But, for instance, you'll discover that students hate a certain book or a certain part of the course. Then you have to think, "Is it because the book is really not appropriate or bad or is it because they don't know what's good for them?" Regardless [of] what conclusion you come up with, if they *really* don't like it then you better do something about it because you know damn well that they are not going to read it [next time].

According to some professors, students simply lacked sufficient expertise to be viewed as qualified evaluators. Others complained that students don't always understand an instructor's purpose and might misinterpret Socratic styles or the "devil's advocate" method as disorganized or confrontational. Still others noted that students can identify the troublesome effect of a teaching problem but cannot understand the cause. An associate professor of mathematics described an incident in her department: students complained about a foreign instructor's language skills, whereas the actual problem was his tendency to provide over-elaborate illustrations in class. Once he simplified his examples, the complaints about his language ability stopped. As the woman professor explained, students' complaints might "signal a problem but don't always tell us the difficulty."

Another evaluation issue common to many respondents in the sample, regardless of gender, was exemplified by the confusing experience of simultaneously receiving highly positive and highly negative evaluations for the same class, text, or even segment of the course. One woman explained:

> One will say, "This is the worst course I ever heard of in my life!" and the very next one you read will say, "I just loved it!" (full, food management).

The jarring effects of such inconsistency were magnified by the virulence of the criticism coupled with the lavishness of the praise, which served as a reminder of the extreme diversity of students' opinions.

> One year I had two comments. One was, "This is the third worst course I have ever taken and it should not be required for an anthropology major, was totally boring, etc." Comment two was "This is one of the best courses I've ever taken" (female associate, linguistics).

> Some of them saying, "You're the best professor I ever had," and some saying the worst . . . This person puts me to sleep." You wonder if it's really the same class they're taking about (male, full, physics).

The result of such experiences with widely divergent evaluations was that many teachers came to question the value of ratings. One of the professors explained his reservations:

> It always concerned me that in the same set of evaluations you'll have people who will see something as being very positive and other people who see exactly that same thing as being very negative. So you begin to question the validity of it [student evaluations] (male, full, education).

In addition to their awareness of the impossibility of pleasing all students, some faculty members recognized that evaluations are colored by a number of other factors beyond the individual teacher's control. Whether the course was a requirement or an elective, the size of the class, class location and time of day, the level of difficulty of the course, the evaluation format required by departmental promotion and tenure committees, and the grade expected by the student were mentioned as extraneous influences on students' evaluations.

Yet teachers also valued the information gained through these evaluations; often they characterized the student as "our client" or as a "consumer" who is perfectly well qualified to describe his or her satisfaction with professional services. Teachers reported that they used students' feedback in a variety of ways, including: (1) modifying bad habits such as talking too fast, looking at the ceiling while lecturing, or being late to class; (2) determining students' interest in the material presented or in particular texts or readers; and (3) gauging students' opinions about the fairness of tests and grading procedures.

In fact, many of the faculty members interviewed said that they used students' feedback selectively to guide them in developing their course content and teaching style. That is, even while they recognized the evaluation process as flawed, teachers reported that they relied on their students because other faculty members in their departments paid little attention to teaching methods and techniques. A male assistant professor in English noted, "People don't usually seem to be that interested; it seems like bragging to say 'I had a great class.'" As a female assistant professor in social science described her department, "In most cases I expect people not to want to hear that (about teaching), to give me negative feedback, to be disinterested." These sentiments, echoed by many of the professors, meant that many university teachers were forced to turn to their students for feedback to improve their teaching quality.

Gender Divergences

Although men and women professors were very similar in their perceptions of the usefulness of evaluations, their accounts differed in two ways: (1) the extent to which women reported that students evaluated their personalities in addition to their teaching effectiveness, and (2) the extent to which men discussed the politics of student evaluations and their effects on promotion and tenure decisions.

Women mentioned repeatedly that student evaluations typically included judgments about their personalities. For example, women professors were criticized for "not smiling enough" in class or for being "dull," or "unexciting," or "too formal." They were complimented for their "relaxed style," "enthusiasm," "openness," or "outgoing" manner. Although one or two of the men mentioned personality as a factor in quality of evaluations, women were much more strongly aware that students were judging their personalities in addition to their professional teaching competency.

The extent to which these judgments of personality were problematic for the women depended on whether their natural mannerisms were those valued by the students. Thus, those women who were interesting, expressive, and open reported approval; those who were reserved, formal, and precise said that they received criticism. Two women in the hard sciences described the latter situation; one reported, "I don't smile enough" and another reported being told, "I'm not dramatic." Yet negative comments on personality appeared across disciplinary boundaries.

Some of the women expressed dismay at having their personalities subjected to evaluation: they felt that this criterion was not applied to their male colleagues. Others felt that because their teaching styles involved the creation of an atmosphere in which students could participate, the degree to which their personalities facilitated such an atmosphere made such evaluations relevant. One assistant professor of English explained:

> I think my personality is relevant in the kind of teaching I do, in eliciting discussion and all that. I don't lecture very often or very much, so I don't find those comments irrelevant at all. I think my personality is very involved in my teaching.

When we consider that women described more personalization in their classrooms and displayed more of these behaviors in our observational results, it is not surprising to find judgments of their personalities appearing in students' accounts of their teaching. The question then becomes whether the women are simply more sensitive to these types of comments or whether students are more likely to make personality judgments when evaluating female professors than when evaluating male professors. The answer can be discerned directly from the student evaluation data discussed in the following section. If students use divergent criteria for male and for female teachers, the inevitable variability in female teaching behavior, hypothesized by the contextual/woman-centered approach, means that some women (as well as some men) will not conform to students' preferences. According to either perspective—woman-centered or role conflict/status inconsistency—women professors would be likely to display more of their personalities to students. The telling difference is in the students' reactions: whether they like women who personalize but judge them to be less competent (as predicted by the role conflict/status inconsistency perspective) or whether they truly prefer this approach, judging them to be both more likable and more competent (as predicted by the woman-centered perspective).

One final difference between the accounts of men and women professors is that the men in our sample tended to be more cognizant of what we call the politics of the student evaluation process. They repeatedly discussed ways in which such evaluations were unfair or unreliable instruments for tenure and promotion decisions. Often they commented that students' evaluations should be for the professors' knowledge and benefit, and not for those above them in the hierarchy. Other respondents felt that poor teachers could manipulate their results on evaluations by giving higher grades, by being "entertaining" in class, and by trying to secure upper-level teaching assignments with fewer freshmen and more advanced students.

In general, the male interviewees were considerably more skeptical than the women about whether students' judgments were useful for anything other than simple client satisfaction information; they questioned the applicability of those judgments in decisions even about tenure and annual salary. As one male assistant professor of history remarked, "No one gets tenure on the basis of good teaching." His sentiments were echoed by other men, who thought that, although bad teaching might hurt chances for advancement, good teaching certainly would not help those chances. In this view, students' evaluations became less powerful as long as a teacher could avoid serious complaints about incompetent teaching. Accordingly, men were able to experience the evaluations as meaningful but could dismiss complaints that they found too threatening or too time-consuming to address. These sentiments echo the feelings voiced by men in discussing teaching methods more generally: they did not perceive students to be true partners in the learning process as often as did the women. (See chapter 3, "Locus of Learning.")

The Professorial Role

Before we consider the students' reactions, it might be helpful to review what they are reacting to. What are the expectations of the professional role? First, let us see what these professors actually do in the classroom. Data obtained from the observations (table 6.1) summarize the time spent on specific activities. They show that much classroom time is spent ordering (8.7 percent) and presenting material (67.4 percent), responding to students questions (8.7 per-

TABLE 6.1

Proportion of Classroom Time Spent in Selected Activities

Basic Instructional Activities	Percentage
Presenting material	67.4
Ordering presentations	8.7
Managerial behaviors	3.6
Responding to questions	8.7
Soliciting clarification	1.3
Checking students' understanding	2.1
Soliciting students' input	3.7
Responses solicited from students	4.3
Experiential presentations and activities	2.0
Professor's and students' thought	0.1
Professor's and students' laughter	1.4
Total students' input	11.8
Students presenting material	2.2
Students' solicitations of information	1.5
Authority Management Behaviors	
Students' challenges	0.3
Students' evaluations	0.2
Students' interruptions	0.2
Professor's positive evaluations	2.2
Professor's negative evaluations	0.6
Professor's unspoken positive reinforcement	0.0
Professor's admonishments	0.2
Professor's ridicule	0.1
Professor's interruptions	0.2
Professor's partial positive evaluations	0.3
Professor's partial negative evaluations	0.1
Personalizations	
Professor's personalizations	2.0
Professor's personalizations related to self	1.3
Professor's personalizations related to students	0.7
Professor expressing empathy for students	0.2
Professor acknowledging students' contributions	1.4
Personalizations by students	0.5

Note: These percentages do not sum to 100 percent. There is some overlap between certain variables, and not all activities are included here.

cent) and soliciting their input (3.7 percent), receiving students' input of all types (11.8 percent), and receiving students' responses to solicitations (4.3 percent). Presenting material is clearly the major activity, but students' input occurs next most frequently. Hence, role behaviors are primarily professor-focused presentations, but a considerable amount of time is spent in seeking and receiving students' input. Expectations apparently involve interaction between student and professor; straight lecturing is not the usual practice.

TABLE 6.2

Differences in Instructors' Behaviors

	Women	*Men*
Eye Contact		
Much	91.7%	82.5%
Little	8.3%	12.5%
Extemporaneous		
Reliance on notes	33.3%	23.7%
Extemporaneous	66.7%	76.2%
Lecture/Discussion		
Mostly lecture	39.6%	60.0%
Mostly discussion	18.8%	12.5%
Mixture	41.7%	27.5%
Classroom Climate		
Formal	37.5%	35.0%
Casual	62.5%	65.0%
Students' Participation[a]		
Many participating	60.4%	42.5%
Few participating	39.6%	57.5%
Students' Talking		
Talking during lectures	18.8%	20.0%
Quiet	81.3%	80.0%
Students' Attentiveness		
Attentive	81.3%	77.5%
Nonattentive	18.8%	22.5%
Lecture Style[a]		
Pleasant, varied, with inflections	91.7%	75.0%
Monotonous	8.3%	25.0%
N	68	90

[a]Gender differences significant, $p < .05$.

Regarding the interactive nature of the role relationship, information taken from cover sheets completed by the observers shows that although students are basically attentive and quiet while the professor lectures, most classrooms have a casual atmosphere in which the professor makes much eye contact, involves students in a mixture of discussion and lecture, and uses extemporaneous material in the process (table 6.2). Formal, dry, prearranged lectures are rare; students' involvement during a significant minority of the classroom time is the norm. How do students react to these behaviors?

Students' Evaluations

Late in the semester, after the observations occurred, the researchers returned and distributed questionnaires to the students in the classes that had been observed. The questionnaires (see appendix D) included five items from the university-designed SET student evaluation commonly used at this university (items 1 to 5), as well as six other items pertinent to the study. Other items further explored perceptions of the professor's competence ("logical presentations") and introduced the topic of control techniques ("too authoritarian") as well as the instructor's likability ("considerate of students," "would like to get to know personally," "responsive to

FIGURE 6.1

Evaluation Items on Student Questionnaire

The instructor was well-prepared for class.
The instructor had a thorough knowledge of the subject.
The instructor communicated the subject matter well.
The instructor stimulated interest in the course subject.
The instructor is one of the best teachers I have known at this university.
The instructor presented the material in a logical manner.
This instructor is responsive to student input.
Sometimes, this instructor seems to be too authortarian.
This instructor was generally very considerate of students.
If given the opportunity, I would like to know this instructor more informally.
Compared to most other female/male instructors, this one is among the best.

TABLE 6.3

Mean Evaluation Scores, by Sex

		Sex of Instructor	
		Males	*Females*
Professor is:			
Competence	1. Prepared	1.49	1.57
	2. Thorough	1.38	1.41
	3. Able to communicate ideas	1.95	2.02
	4. Stimulating	2.08	2.08
	5. One of the best instructors	2.52	2.47
	6. Logical	2.00	2.02
Likability	7. Responsive to students	1.89	1.83
	8. Too authoritarian	3.55	3.56
	9. Considerate of students	1.85	1.82
	10. Someone I would like to know informally	2.36	2.21
	11. One of the best same-sex instructors	2.38	2.25

Note: None of these sex differences is statistically significant. In all cases p > .2, usually much larger.

students"). Students rated their professors from 1 (strongly agree) to 5 (strongly disagree) on all items. (See appendix D for the complete survey instrument.)

In general, students gave high ratings to both men and women professors; the average rating on most items fell between strongly agree (1) and agree (2), and none fell below neutral (3) or average. Students apparently felt that their professors (men and women) were both competent *and* likable. (See table 6.3.) Then we summed various combinations of these items into separate competence and likability scales for men and for women professors. (See appendix C for the factor analysis results that form the basis for the construction of these scales.)

Students' Reactions to Teaching Behaviors

Basic Instructional Activities

As we observed in chapter 3, women professors made stronger attempts than men to involve students in the classroom process and received more student input. How were these efforts received by the students? The answer is mixed (table 6.4).[1] Some attempts to involve students lowered their evaluations; others raised them.

We also found differences in the direction of effects for evaluations of men and of women professors; this finding suggests that students might hold different expectations or perceptions of the two sexes. For instance, the more classroom time a woman professor spent in presenting material, the lower her likability ratings, but the reverse was true for the men professors. Perhaps students expect women to yield more classroom time to them, but admire men who hold forth as experts. Indeed, the amount of time students spent in responding to solicitations and laughing with their women professors enhanced both competence and likability ratings, whereas the total amount of time men professors gave to students' input (solicited responses, total students' input, students presenting material) lowered their likability ratings. Checking students' understanding and soliciting their input also enhanced the women's competence ratings but had a strong negative impact on both competence and likability ratings for men. Because these behaviors are ways in which men and women professors differ in basic teaching style, one might conclude that women do more often what their students reward them for doing, while men professors avoid activities that will be sanctioned negatively. Professors and students also might hold similar expectations for men and for women professors; perhaps the students are simply expressing their preferences, and perhaps the professors would act in this way regardless of students' reactions. Our theory, however, argues that there is a causal effect.

Students seem to have a clear sense of what they expect from each gender. For example, certain behaviors that are more characteristic of the women professors tend to lower their evaluations. The more solicitations of students, the lower the women professors' competence ratings. The same is true for the proportion of time spent in responding to questions. Although students generally seem to enjoy women's interactive style, they seem to perceive certain limits and to see specific behaviors as signaling less competence. "If I have to ask a *woman* professor to clarify something, does that mean *she* hasn't clarified it clearly enough?" a student might wonder. Women tend to blame themselves for difficulties; perhaps others also blame women and not themselves. Although more research is needed to understand the meaning of this finding, it appears that classes in which students frequently question the woman professor are experienced by the students as less satisfying.

TABLE 6.4

Effects of Basic Instructional Activities on Students' Evaluations of
Professors' Competence and Likability, by Sex

	Women Professors		Men Professors	
	Competence	Likability	Competence	Likability
Structured Presentations				
Managerial behaviors	.139*	.038	.011	.107*
Presentation of material	−.025	−.290**	.102	.182**
Other miscellaneous (correcting self, manipulating artifacts)	−.071	−.051	.148*	.097
Mild Efforts to Involve Students				
Responding to questions	−.243**	−.089	−.045	−.075
Soliciting clarification	−.030	−.046	−.011	−.158*
Checking students' understanding	.145*	.119	−.122*	−.243***
Strong Efforts to Involve Students				
Soliciting students' input	−.235**	−.187	−.093	−.102
Responses solicited from students	.179*	.144*	−.088	−.109*
Experiential presentations and activities	−.001	−.002	.050	−.031
Professors' and students' thought	−.006	.008	.003	−.007
Professors' and students' laughter	.165*	.356***	.036	.029
Students' Involvement				
Total students' input	.038	.119	−.052	−.150*
Students presenting material	−.013	.061	.013	−.116*
Students' solicitations of information	−.352***	−.080	.087	.062

Note: Partial correlations controlling for class size, proportion of class that is
female, male domination of professor's department (1 = male-dominated).

***Significant at the .001 level.
**Significant at the .01 level.
*Significant at the .05 level.

Authority Management and Personalizations

The effects of authority management (table 6.5)[1] and personalizing (table 6.6)[1] behaviors are much more straightforward. As for authority management techniques, women were seen as more likable, the more interruptions they received from students; they also were seen as less competent, though not significantly so. In addition, women were judged more likable, the more partial positive and

TABLE 6.5

Effects of Authority Management Techniques on Students' Assessments of Professors' Competence and Likability, by Sex

	Women Professors		Men Professors	
Students' Aggressiveness	Competence	Likability	Competence	Likability
Challenges	−.138	−.159	.079	−.039
Evaluations	.129	.080	−.064	−.124*
Interruptions	−.115	.213**	.070	−.041
Professor Evaluating				
Positive evaluations	.033	.071	−.028	−.047
Negative evaluations	.095	.045	.095	.149*
Unspoken positive reinforcement	−.335***	−.187*	.072	−.027
Harsh/Direct Control Techniques				
Admonishments	.115	.0477	.060	.120*
Ridicule	.143*	.037	−.041	.032
Professor interrupting student	−.114	−.008	.100	.132*
Modified Control Techniques				
Partial positive evaluations	.133	.238**	.097	.058
Partial negative evaluations	.277**	.224**	−.046	−.062

Note: Partial correlations controlling for class size, proportion of class that is female, male domination of professor's department (1 = male-dominated).

***Significant at the .001 level.
**Significant at the .01 level.
*Significant at the .05 level.

TABLE 6.6

Effects of Personalizing on Students' Assessments of Professors'
Competence and Likability, by Sex

	Women Professors		Men Professors	
	Competence	Likability	Competence	Likability
Professor's Personal- *ization*	.185*	.132	.109*	.110*
Related to self	.063	.090	.031	.051
Related to students	.251**	.115	.128*	.108*
Professor's Expression				
Empathy for students	.127	.149	−.048	.002
Acknowledgment of students' contribu- tions	.259**	.406***	−.096	−.230**
Students' Personal- *izations*	.111	.157	−.147*	−.111*

Note: Partial correlations controlling for class size, proportion of class that
is female, male domination of professor's department (1 = male-
dominated).

***Significant at the .001 level.
**Significant at the .01 level.
*Significant at the .05 level.

negative evaluations they gave to students. They were seen as more
competent the more time they spent in giving partial negative evaluations. Apparently students appreciated women professors who
demonstrated their control of both classroom and subject matter in
an interactive, qualified fashion. These women were deemed more
competent even when they engaged in ridicule. This happened
rarely (table 4.3), however, so this finding might not be as meaningful. At any rate, we found no evidence that students resent women
professors who take and use their authority, as long as they do so
interactively. Interestingly, women are judged less competent and
less likable the more unspoken positive reinforcement (mostly head
nodding) they give; again, however, this happened rarely and so
should not be overemphasized.

None of these behaviors affected the men's competence ratings.
Their likability ratings were enhanced by their use of negative evaluations, admonishments, and interruptions. Apparently students

prefer or expect these types of interactions from their male professors. Yet students' aggressiveness in the classroom (students making evaluative statements) served to lower the men's ratings of competence. Students seem to dislike men who allow them to assume the locus of control in this way.

Personalizations enhanced the women's competence and likability ratings uniformly, although the results are not always statistically significant. The strongest effects are seen for women's acknowledgment of students' contributions and for personalizations related specifically to students. Bringing the student personally into the learning process enhances students' positive ratings of women professors.

This is not consistently the case for the men, however. Male professors' personalizations, especially those relating course material specifically to the students' lives, had positive effects on both competence and likability ratings. Acknowledging students and the incidence of students' personalizations, however, actually had negative effects on students' ratings of male professors. Aside from the use of examples from the students' lives to make the material relevant in class, the students apparently were uncomfortable when a male professor deferred to or acknowledged a student's contribution or "allowed" students to talk about their personal lives. Again, students might perceive these male professors as lacking control over the classroom or as deviating from their gender role.

Summary

This pattern of results reinforces the findings in the previous chapters that suggest the existence of different teaching models for men and for women. There we found the two sexes behaving differently in the professorial role. Here we find the two types of behaviors rewarded differentially. Women professors were rated more highly when they used a more interactive teaching model that permitted student input; monopolizing the limelight for their own presentations received strong negative sanctions. Men professors, on the other hand, were sanctioned more consistently for receiving student input of any type, but particularly personal input; they were reinforced for occupying center stage and for giving negative feedback in the form of admonishments, negative evaluations, and interruptions. Women, though apparently rewarded for interacting with students on a more personal level, nonetheless were expected to maintain control with their interactive method (giving partial positive and negative evaluations, for instance) and were sanctioned for interactive techniques that might signal lack of control (e.g., receiving many questions and solicitations from students).

Data from the interviews revealed that faculty members' perceptions of these evaluations were basically accurate. Students evaluated female professors more positively when the women used an interactive teaching style and involved their personalities in the learning process. In contrast, male professors' opinion that they, not the students, were the real experts in the classroom was confirmed by the fact that students judged the male teachers more positively when they spent a large proportion of class time presenting material, and more negatively when the amount of input by students was high. Overall, we could say that the two approaches seemed to be equally effective, at least so far as student assessments are concerned.

The professors' confusion—their feeling that they received simultaneous positive and negative evaluations—becomes more understandable when we consider some of the inconsistencies in the students' reactions. For example, women were rewarded (with better evaluations) for allowing students to occupy class time with their insights (students' responses to solicitations), but were punished (with poor evaluations) when students spent a larger proportion of time asking questions. Similarly, although men were evaluated more positively when they used examples from students' lives to illustrate points in class, they also were judged more negatively when they encouraged direct student participation.

 These apparent inconsistencies may stem from the failure of both male and female professors to perceive fine distinctions in teaching style that might be readily evident to the students. In other words, while a female professor wonders why her attempt to involve students in the classroom is applauded by some and scorned by others, her students might feel that such an interactive style indicates a lack of competence in subject matter; they might be suspicious of her efforts to encourage participation but might enjoy the end result, namely involvement by students. Similarly, a man trying to reduce the distance from his students by devoting more classroom time to them might find himself sanctioned negatively by those very students for "forcing" a half-hearted interactive style.

Thus far, our study has uncovered of a variety of processes interpreted from a number of viewpoints by persons involved in university learning. What does it all mean? Can the different findings be integrated? What are the practical implications of these results? We turn to these questions in the next and final chapter.

Conclusions and Implications for Teachers and Administrators

This study draws upon recent developments in role theory and feminist analysis to examine and interpret the behavior and perceptions of men and women university professors, as well as their students' responses. Accordingly, our study provides an opportunity to synthesize these recent theoretical developments and to evaluate their relative explanatory power.

The status inconsistency/role conflict perspective, derived from structural role theory, posits dualistic assumptions about males' and females' behavior and attitudes. Males are seen as incorporating different traits and acting in different ways from females; these differences are interpreted as sex-typed. When women are placed in situations that are sex-typed male, the perspective argues, they experience status inconsistency because their female sex status is inconsistent with their occupational status of professor. Women also experience extreme role conflict in such situations because the demands of the two different roles (such as female and professor) are contradictory and divergent; the role demands exist as structural imperatives not amenable to change by the individual. As a result, structural role theory predicts that women professors will encounter difficulty functioning in the traditionally male-dominated occupational world of academia, and that their female sex-typed behaviors will detract from their competence. Although perhaps this perspective overstates the existence of stereotypical gender differences, it contributes the valuable insight of the double bind.

Interactionist (cf. Stryker and Macke 1978; Stryker and Statham 1985; Turner 1978, 1975) and contextual/feminist modifications to this perspective (cf. Gerson and Peiss 1985; Thorne and Luria 1986) emphasize the agency of the individual. From these perspectives, the individual is not only responding to a set of role demands and experiencing role conflict but also has some power to affect the situation and to negotiate understandings, changing role demands in the process. Accordingly, one of the understandings that individuals can negotiate is how their gender will be articulated and how this articulation should be evaluated and interpreted. Thus, behavior, including teaching behavior, is situational and is negotiated in particular contexts. Different aspects of the situation will affect the negotiation; in the case of teaching, the management of power and authority is crucial. Further, because the display and the evaluation are situated contextually, women professors can use their gender to strengthen their position in the classroom and to defuse rather than to generate problems.

The interactionist perspective contends that although males' and females' teaching styles may differ, the sharp division by sex proposed by the more structural version of status inconsistency/role conflict does not exist in all cases. Males and females might, on some measures, be more similar than dissimilar. This was certainly the case among the full professors we interviewed; they gave evidence that features of the context other than gender can affect the enactment of gender roles. Further, if there are female sex-typed teaching behaviors, they might not be deprecated but might be evaluated positively by students and become a major strength for the women involved.

In addition to these insights based on the interactionist perspective, including feminist versions, we incorporate a contribution that comes only from the women-centered feminist literature. That contribution—the recognition of the importance of the relationship in framing interaction—provides a major mechanism used to negotiate role relationships, making the situation more congruent for all parties involved regardless of any existing conflict or inconsistency. In this situation we see women in particular attempting to create and nurture a certain type of relationship with students that—from the women's perspective—enhances their ability to teach effectively. It allows students to become more independent learners and to integrate their new knowledge with their personal experiences.

Summary of Findings

What We Expected

As discussed in chapter 3, we anticipated finding few gender differences in basic teaching approaches. The structuring of material, checking students' understanding, and minimal use of the participatory method are essential aspects of basic postsecondary instructional activities and are expected to be found in most college and university teaching settings. Other behaviors, such as authority management and personalizing are more situational and might reflect gender role portrayals more sensitively.

Beyond providing structure and assuring students' understanding, women professors were expected to differ from men professors in the way they managed their classrooms. We expected these differences to arise from three sources: (1) a woman's attempt to manage the role conflict/status inconsistency inherent in her situation by "cooling out" resentment through avoidance of the "pushy" or "uppity woman" label; (2) a woman's attempt to negotiate role demands so that she could enact the professorial role in a way more in keeping with her own—and her students'—preferences and expectations for "appropriate" feminine behavior; and (3) a woman's focus on the nature of the relationship formed between herself and her role partners, which she could employ as a mechanism for negotiating comfortable role expectations and executing them to her own satisfaction. All of these factors may operate simultaneously.

On the basis of this reasoning, we expected women to make greater use of participatory teaching methods involving students as more equal partners in the classroom. We expected that they would establish their authority in the classroom by using methods that simultaneously enhanced their authority and reduced the appearance of authority. We expected that both women professors and their students would use more personalizations by encouraging the contribution of personal material and applying it to individual lives. We expected a successful outcome for female professors' attempts at role alignment and an acceptance of these negotiated understandings on the part of students. Finally, we expected that these differences might not hold for professors at all ranks, particularly full professors given that individuals modify their roles over time.

What We Found

Our results show the utility of each theoretical perspective in accounting for gender differences and similarities in behavior and attitudinal patterns: especially evident is the robustness of recently modified structural role theory, which shares the power of both interactionism and contextual women-centered approaches. Before turning to our theoretical interpretations, we summarize briefly what we found.

Basic instructional activities. As evident in both the interview and the observational data, we found few gender differences regarding the salience of teaching or the use of basic instructional techniques. Both men and women professors spent much of their classroom time presenting material; they were equally likely to use managerial practices, to correct themselves, and to use teaching aids. Further, there were no observed gender differences in the "tightness" or "looseness" of the classroom structure, though women reported their students to be somewhat less tolerant of a looser structure (table 7.1).

We found striking differences, however, in the emphasis of teaching for men and for women. Women tended to focus more on the student as the locus of learning; men, on themselves. Although both sexes claimed to use an interactive style, women did so more extensively, taking more pains to involve students and to receive more input from students. Men used as many of the milder efforts to involve students as did women (responding to questions and soliciting students' clarification, but not checking students' understanding), while women used more of the stronger efforts (soliciting and receiving input, using experiential learning, providing time to think and contemplate). In keeping with these observations, women placed more emphasis on students' participation. They reported that their teaching satisfaction came from students relating to each other, developing their own ideas, and coming prepared to participate in class discussions. Men tended to regard students' participation as a requirement or sometimes as a "time waste" ("throw[ing] away a period just talking," "chattering about the material"). For the women, particularly the assistant professors, who were still highly invested in teaching, conveying the content to the students was central, whereas the men tended to concentrate on instructional methods and techniques. The women reported forming personal, individual relationships with their students. Even the women full professors, who were less invested in teaching at this stage in their careers, reported letting students move with agendas of their own and trying not to talk down to them. The women's efforts to nurture independent thinkers seemed to be successful; we observed students presenting material of their own more often and independently soliciting more information in women's than men's classrooms.

Rank also affected these patterns; this was however, particularly evident in the interview results. Women full professors were less invested in their teaching; they resembled the men full professors more closely than they resembled the women assistant or

TABLE 7.1

Summary of Gender Differences in Teaching Styles: Basic Instructional Activities

Basic Instruction	By Women More Often	By Men More Often	No Difference
	Behaviors Engaged In or Factors Stressed		
Salience of teaching			*
Presentation of material[b]			*
Managerial behaviors			*
Miscellaneous structuring			*
Tight or loose structure			*
Perception that students resent loose structure	*		
Focus on:			
Conveying content	*[a]		
Exciting students	*[a]		
Interacting with students	*[a]		
Methods of teaching		*	
Doing the teaching		*	
Mild Efforts to Involve Students			
Responding to questions			*
Soliciting clarification			*
Checking student understanding	*		
Strong Efforts to Involve Students			
Soliciting students' input[b]	*		
Receiving solicited responses	*		
Experiential learning	*		
Thinking, contemplating	*		
Laughter			*
Claimed use of interactive format			*
Students' participation as necessary for learning	*		
Student as locus of learning	*		
Students' participation as motivating technique			*
Total students' input	*		
Students presenting material[b]	*		
Students' solicitations of information[b]	*		

[a]Woman full professors were less likely to stress these factors.
[b]Sex interacted with tenure in regression equation.

associate professors. The same pattern was suggested in the observation data, where women full professors seemed to make less use of the participatory model, but we did not have a sufficient number of women full professors to permit a reliable statistical test of this pattern.

Authority management. In the interviews, women talked a great deal about the need to establish their authority (particularly their credibility) in the classroom. Men more often discussed a need to reduce their authority or to reduce the distance between themselves and their students. We observed no differences in students' tendency to challenge, interrupt, or evaluate their professors. (These things seldom happened to professors of either sex.) The two sexes, however, displayed their authority differently. Women, particularly assistant professors, felt that they had to handle challenges to their authority very carefully. They more often ignored the student, talked to him or her privately, or attempted to respond humorously or in an offhand manner. (Women full professors reported dealing with these situations much more directly and more quickly.) Men reported themselves as less hesitant to reprimand directly, harshly, and publicly; indeed, we observed that they were slightly more likely to use ridicule in their classrooms.

Women professors used certain techniques that simultaneously legitimated their authority and reduced their appearance of authority. Although they yielded the floor more often to their students, they made use of student-professor interaction to give more corrective feedback, both positive and negative. They also gave more partial positive feedback, which we speculate might have been their way of delivering negative feedback in a gentler fashion. They also established their authority by giving more admonishments, many of them managerial. These findings are summarized in table 7.2.

Some of these patterns were moderated by the effect of rank. Women full professors were less hesitant to use direct, confrontational techniques to resolve challenges to authority; again, this pattern is more similar to that of the men full professors than to that of the other women. As before, the observation data suggested a similar pattern, but the number of women full professors was too small to permit a reliable test.

Personalizations. Clear gender differences existed in personalizing behaviors. Women personalized more often in the classroom, divulging information about themselves slightly more often and talking about personal issues in their students' lives much more often. The interviews revealed that although men talked about themselves, they more often discussed their career histories or work-related topics.

This difference is illustrated most clearly by a woman who said "[I try to] reach students where they live . . . as a way of understanding [the class material]." The women often saw personalizing as a way of building bridges between the students' experiences and the material. Men more often saw personalizing as "a duty" or a "presentation of credentials." The women professors also were more likely to acknowledge students' contributions; concomitantly, their students were more likely to personalize in their classrooms. Women reported more interaction with students outside the classroom, particularly more chatting and more counseling. Men, on the other hand, reported engaging in more grade negotiations outside of class with their students (table 7.2).

The personalizing behaviors reported in the interviews did not differ by rank, though several interactions appeared in the observation data. Again, however, the numbers of women full professors were too small to permit a reliable statistical test.

Students' reactions. Students rated their men and women professors as equally effective instructors. For the most part, adherence to the gender-appropriate model was rewarded with higher evaluations. Women's competence ratings were higher the more they interacted with students by checking students' understanding, personalizing, acknowledging students' contributions, giving partial negative feedback, soliciting students' input, responding to students' requests for information or material, and generating laughter in the classroom. Women faculty also were viewed as more competent the more they engaged in managerial behaviors. Interestingly, their competence ratings were higher if they engaged in a greater amount of ridicule (though this behavior occurred rarely). As with competence, women's likability ratings increased the more they interacted with students by generating laughter, acknowledging students' contributions, responding to students' requests for information or material, being interrupted by students, and giving partial positive and negative feedback.

Women were more disliked the less they interacted with students and presented material. They were judged less competent the more classroom occurrences indicated problems in communicating

TABLE 7.2

Summary of Gender Differences in Teaching Styles:
Authority Management and Personalizations

	Behaviors Engaged in or Factors Stressed		
Authority Management	By Women More Often	By Men More Often	No Difference
Perceived need to establish authority	*a		
Perceived need to reduce authority		*a	
Students' challenges			*
Students' evaluations of correctness			*
Students' interruptions			*
Handled Challenges by:			
Ignoring	*b		
Talking to student privately	*b		
Public reprimand/ embarrassment		*	
Offhand comment	*b		
Point proved outside class		*	
Positive feedback[c]	*		
Negative feedback[c]	*		
Partial positive feedback	*		
Admonishing	*		
Ridiculing		*	
Interrupting students			*
Personalizations			
Personalizing:	*		
About self[c]			*
About students[c]	*		
Giving career-related information about self		*	
Giving personal information about self	*		
Empathy for students			*
Acknowledging student contributions[c]	*		
Students' personalizations	*		
Chatting outside class	*		
Talking with students about personal problems	*		
Negotiating about grades		*	
Students' Evaluations			
Competence of professor			*
Likability of professor			*

[a]Difference is less true of full professors.

[b]Women full professors dealt with challenges more directly.

[c]Sex interacted with tenure in regression equation.

the material: responding to students' questions, receiving solicitations from students, and (surprisingly) giving unspoken positive reinforcement (though this behavior occurred rarely).

Men's competence ratings were higher the more they adhered to a masculine sex-typed style in structuring their classroom activities. They also were seen as more competent the more they used personalizations related to students. Their likability ratings increased the more they used their typical "teacher as expert" style: presenting material, engaging in managerial behaviors, giving negative corrective feedback, admonishing and interrupting their students, and (surprisingly) engaging in personalizations related to students.

Men were more disliked the more they interacted with students by soliciting clarification from students, checking their understanding, responding to their requests for information or material, and acknowledging their contributions. Their likability ratings also fell the more total student input they received, particularly when students made evaluative statements, presented material, or personalized in their classrooms. This latter variable also lowered men's competence ratings, as did checking students' understanding (table 7.3).

The Structural Role Conflict/Status Inconsistency Perspective

Many of the gender differences we found can be interpreted from the structural role conflict/status inconsistency perspective. The behaviors characteristic of women may have arisen from the role conflict they experienced. In the interviews many women professors, especially assistant professors, spoke of a double bind, as would be predicted by this perspective. They expressed concern with downplaying their femininity lest they be viewed as weak or incompetent. At the same time, they were very much concerned with students as total persons and wanted to relate to them as such. Thus, they used some strategies that increased their appearance of authority and others that decreased it. They seemed to be compelled to engage simultaneously in contradictory behaviors.

According to the structural perspective, women professors feel required to adopt an interactive, affective approach to teaching, partially because of prior socialization and partially because of perceived role pressures and students' demands to conform to more traditional sex-typed behavior. Yet they also perceive that they will be judged as incompetent if they do so. Consequently, a great deal of

TABLE 7.3

Summary of Student Reactions to Women and Men Professors'
Teaching Styles

Women Professors

Behaviors that

Increased competence ratings	Managerial behaviors, checking students' understanding, soliciting student input, responses solicited from students, laughter, partial negative corrective feedback, ridicule, personalizations related to students, acknowledging students' contributions
Increased likability ratings	Soliciting students' input, solicited responses from students, laughter, students' interruptions, partial corrective feedback, acknowledging students' contributions
Decreased competence ratings	Responding to students' questions, students' solicitations, unspoken reinforcement
Decreased likability ratings	Presenting material, unspoken reinforcement

Men Professors

Behaviors that

Increased competence ratings	Miscellaneous structuring activities, personalizations related to students
Increased likability ratings	Managerial behaviors, negative corrective feedback, admonishments, interrupting students, personalizations related to students
Decreased competence ratings	Checking students' understanding, students' personalizations
Decreased likability ratings	Soliciting clarification, checking student understanding, responses solicited from students, total student input, students presenting material, students' corrective feedback, acknowledging students' contributions, students' personalizations

role conflict and status anxiety are generated. Women faculty resolve this situation by supplementing their teaching with behaviors that both assert their authority and "humanize" it.

According to role conflict/status inconsistency reasoning, women are considered warm, nurturant, and supportive (Lewis 1972; McKee 1959; Sherriffs and Farrett, 1953). These expectations might conflict with those for the university professor (directive, assertive, knowledgeable), and thus might lead to the prediction that women will assert their authority indirectly, avoiding harsh and aggressive stances, or will attempt to personalize their teaching situation by incorporating their personal experiences and those of their students into classroom interaction. These strategies permit a woman to adhere more closely to traditional female role expectations while enacting the highly prestigious role of university professor. This is a balancing act that men do not have to master because most traditional male role requirements mesh neatly with the "professor" role.

Further, women may have a more difficult time establishing their competence because women often are assumed to be less competent than men (Hartley 1969; McKee 1959; Pheterson, Kiesler, and Goldberg 1971). According to this perspective, then, women professors might be faced with the necessity of underplaying their authority and at the same time unequivocally demonstrating their competence. The difficulty lies deeper, however. Not only must women perform two seemingly contradictory behaviors at the same time (demonstrating competence and underplaying authority); one type of behavior also might interfere with the other, creating a double bind. Consequently, women who succeed in de-emphasizing their authority may be judged as nonlegitimate, incompetent holders of their professorial position.

The chain of double binds predicted by this perspective suggests that women will not be regarded as legitimate holders of the position "university professor," in view of their basic status as "female." To be regarded as legitimate they must adopt "masculine" sex-typed styles of interaction, which in turn lead to resentment and punishment by students (cf. Kanter 1977). To moderate these interactions, they must increase their "feminine" sex-typed behaviors. By doing so, however, they are judged incompetent and, once again, as nonlegitimate actors in the role of university professor. Men professors, on the other hand, should not experience these conflicts because the status "professor" is consistent with the status "male." Instead they experience a different kind of difficulty, namely overcoming the role distance between themselves and students. Thus, we would expect them to enact their role differently from women.

From this perspective, women's different strategies, such as personalizing, can be interpreted as ways to avoid possible resentment among students by "feminizing" their teaching style. We would expect women professors to reduce their appearance of power in the classroom (by avoiding harsh or direct use of that power) and to personalize their classroom interactions (by creating classroom environments that are warm, caring, and human). Further, we would expect women professors to act simultaneously to assert their legitimacy in the classroom and to demonstrate competency by adhering somewhat more closely than men to behaviors considered to be good teaching, particularly by involving students in the classroom and by asserting their evaluative authority more often (e.g., by making judgments about the correctness of students' responses). The women, indeed, engaged in all of these behaviors. In this sense the role conflict/status inconsistency perspective helps us to understand some of the gender differences we found in teaching styles. Even so, this perspective does not account for all of the differences we found; nor does it account for the *absence* of differences or for the students' reactions, viewed as a whole and in context.

Interactionist Role Theory and the Contextual/ Women-Centered Perspective

The interactionist version of role theory argues that role partners have considerable agency in negotiating and modifying role expectations in particular situations, thus eliminating or managing much of the conflict or misunderstandings that might exist. Recent feminist revisions of gender theory, based largely upon this body of thought, focus on the creation and maintenance of relationships as a major mechanism used by women in role negotiation. These two insights enable us to understand more fully our entire set of findings. In particular, we can account for (1) cases in which men and women behave in the same manner, (2) the extent to which women focus on their relationships with students in all aspects of the teaching behaviors we have examined, and (3) students' apparent acceptance of both teaching styles.

From this perspective we can acknowledge that any gender differences that exist could enable both men and women to accomplish the same goals. Indeed, it might be easier for men and women to accomplish the same goals if they use different techniques. Communicating with students, for example, is a goal of professors. Women's reputed emphasis on relationships might result in a teaching approach that emphasizes relating to the students and interacting with them as a way of communicating the material. This is what we found. Regardless of disciplinary orientation, class size, or course level, the women professors spent significantly more of their classroom time responding and listening to their students or drawing them into the learning process as active participants. Women talked about their personal lives in the classroom and encouraged students to do the same. Their purpose was pedagogical; they saw personalizing as a way of helping the students relate to and learn the material. These women also spoke about their concern for their students and their relationships with them—not as ends in themselves, but as an integral part of the learning process. The women professors used their interpersonal skills as mechanisms for transmitting knowledge, something their male counterparts did only in a very perfunctory manner. Although both sexes were concerned with communicating the material, males believed that they accomplished this goal simply through imparting the information and finding ways to reinforce the subject matter rather than the learners. Thus, the same goal was accomplished through different behaviors by males and by females.

Gender Differences in Teaching Styles

In the three areas of teaching behaviors we studied—basic instructional activities, authority management, and personalizing in the classroom—women differed from men in ways consistent with the expectations arising from the interactionist and recently developed feminist perspectives on roles and gender.

Basic instructional activities. In many ways the two sexes were more similar than we had originally expected. Similarities were most apparent in basic instructional activities; here we found equal levels of commitment to teaching in general and similarities in specific teaching behaviors. Both sexes were likely to structure their presentations and to spend most of the classroom time lecturing, with a fair amount of time given to students' participation. Our interviews, however, revealed a gender difference in attitudes toward students that also was evident in the observational data; women professors were more likely to relate to students as full partners in the learning process. They believed more often than men that students' participation was an essential element of the learning process; consequently, they involved students quite extensively in classroom interaction. Men professors, on the other hand, believed more often that they were the primary (or sole) source of learning in the classroom, and that, while students' participation fulfilled a motivational function, participation was not substantively important. As a result, male professors used the participatory teaching model much more sparingly than female professors. Their interaction with students tended to be minimal; they "called on" students for the "correct" answer, asked whether they had any questions, and answered their questions. Male professors were less likely than women to go beyond these steps to involve students in the learning process. In contrast, women professors provided students with a broader range of learning experiences through classroom participation. They involved students in the learning process at yet another level; they gave their students more classroom time. This tendency among women professors might arise from the fact that women were tied more affectively to their students and were more concerned that their students achieve intellectual *independence*, as shown by our interviews.

Authority management. Women professors also allocated some of their authority to their students; students were found to participate more assertively in the women-taught classrooms. Women professors, however, did not capitulate to students simply by relinquishing all authority. Although they might have yielded some authority, they also asserted their authority, particularly their right to judge the correctness or incorrectness of students' input. Hence, women professors were simultaneously increasing and decreasing their appearance of authority in the classroom through their interactions with students. Both interview and observational data also suggest that women were quite hesitant to use harsh, directly confrontational means of establishing their authority. Instead they used much less confrontational and less direct methods to handle challenges to their competency. From a structural perspective, this tendency is interpreted as representing status insecurity, a desire to "cool out" students who might resent highly placed women. From the alternative perspectives, this tendency is interpreted as an attempt to nurture a certain type of role relationship for the purpose of managing the role (teaching) more effectively.

Personalizing in the classroom. The alternative interpretations are supported further by the fact that women professors went beyond merely refraining from harsh control techniques in their efforts to establish a warm classroom atmosphere. They made active attempts to relate to their students in a personal way. Our interview data suggest that they talked more about personal lives and problems with students, both inside and outside the classroom. When men talked about themselves, they tended to discuss their careers and credentials rather than more intimate topics such as family life or emotional experiences. In addition, male professors scrupulously avoided counseling students about their personal problems.

Our observational data also revealed women's tendency toward more personalizing in the classroom. More classroom time was spent in sharing personal experiences, especially those of the students; women professors engaged in more behaviors showing concern and respect for students, such as acknowledging students' contributions personally and positively.

In sum, certain gender differences evident in these findings can be explained by the interactionist and the contextual/woman-centered perspectives. Gender differences appeared and could be seen as positive examples of women using dissimilar but effective methods of accomplishing desired goals. Women professors seemed to take a more person-oriented, student-centered approach to teaching. They were more deeply concerned with the emotional atmosphere in the classroom, with students as total persons, and with involving students extensively in the learning process. Their strategies reduced role distance and enhanced the student-centeredness of their classrooms. This difference in orientation was evident in both the interview and the observational data. This is not to imply that the women were unconcerned with conveying material adequately; on the contrary, they used the same strategies as the males to structure their presentations, to correct students' mistakes, and to check students' understanding. In some cases they were actually more likely to do this kind of structuring. Yet they had a wider range of approaches from which to draw in accomplishing this instrumental goal; they employed their person-oriented skills to convey the material effectively. The women also were more likely to give positive and negative feedback to their students. As a result they were not simply abdicating their authority positions for the sake of establishing an emotionally supportive classroom atmosphere; they took and used their professorial authority interactively with students.

Rank as a situational factor. The interactionist perspective also can account for the *absence* of differences that we found. Recognizing the authority inherent in the professorial role, we might expect similarities in specific teaching behaviors. Perhaps women faculty members are not expected to conform totally to stereotypic role expectations for women, given the demands of the immediate situation. Indeed, we found that rank was a situational factor that accounted for lack of differences. Women with higher rank, who had acquired tenure and, hence, were more independent, exhibited less of the gender-differentiated teaching style that characteristized the assistant professors. In fact, their styles resembled the student-divested style more characteristic of associate and senior men.

This trend, evident in the interviews but not (for sampling reasons) in the observations, requires further scrutiny in future research. None of our data make clear why it occurs. Perhaps only those women who are "correctly" socialized professionally—and who adopt styles more similar to men's—achieve tenure. Perhaps a general maturation effect occurs for both sexes—as in many professions—whereby individuals decrease their interpersonal rapport with clients (or students) after years in their fields. It also may be that professorial rank and status are apparent to students as well as to colleagues, and women full professors are given more independence from common role expectations. Perhaps the style more characteristic of women is viewed as more becoming and more accepted in *younger* women, or perhaps tenure affords a woman the luxury of showing her true feelings. (This latter possibility, however, seems particularly unlikely in view of the enthusiasm, even passion, with which women assistant professors spoke of their commitment to students.) Possibly, we are observing a cohort or period effect, in which new generations of professors view their role differently from earlier generations. Whatever the reason, the interactionist perspective of role theory accounts more readily for our findings related to academic rank and provides a theoretical basis for exploring the academic hierarchy more thoroughly. The structural role conflict/status inconsistency perspective might lead us to expect stereotypic sex-typed differences throughout a career, in which women continue to feel uneasy in their double-bind situations regardless of rank.

Students' Reactions

According to all of the perspectives from which we are drawing interpretively, individuals behave as they do largely because of significant others' influence, in this case because students strongly sanction (resent) women who fail to meet role expectations. We have the data to test this assertion. We measured student reactions along two dimensions: competence and likability ratings. According to the structural role theory perspective, students (1) will approve of women who underplay their authority but will view them as less competent, and (2) will judge as competent those women who assert their legitimacy. Perhaps students like women who assert their legitimacy in ways that involve interacting with students (especially through use of the participatory teaching model.)

Did the strategies that women used reduce these conflicts? Not by their own accounts. Young women professors who used authority-reduction techniques (and young men professors, to some extent) continued to experience a great deal of conflict. Higher ranking women professors reported less conflict, but they had lessened considerably their student-centered approach to teaching. In fact, female full professors had begun to take a more utilitarian approach (much like their male colleagues) and saw themselves, not their students, as the locus of learning.

We also can gain insight into this conflict by looking directly at students' reactions to different professors, as elicited by the process of student evaluation. According to the interviews, students are an important source of untenured women professors' sense of worth and competence. Moreover, student evaluations at this university are somewhat influential in determining the women's (and men's) chances for success in the university. From the structural perspective, some of these teaching strategies should have had quite strong and specific effects on students' evaluations. Students would be expected to like women professors who reduce their appearance of authority, personalize, and show concern for effectively conveying information, and should dislike women professors who use harsh control techniques. Some of these strategies—effectively conveying material and assertion of authority—should enhance students' assessments of their professors' competence, while others—reduction of authority and personalizing—might lower assessments of competence (perhaps, though, while simultaneously enhancing corresponding assessments of likability).

From the interactionist and the contextual/woman-centered perspectives, students might not be pressuring women professors to negotiate such stereotypic, contradictory expectations. Instead, the individual agency that all actors possess in the situation might enable students and professors to negotiate role behaviors that are comfortable to both parties. In this case, gender differences in approaches to teaching may be recognized, accepted, and possibly even rewarded by students. These perspectives do not predict that students uniformly and automatically will derogate women's approaches by applying a stereotypic cultural bias, nor that women necessarily will be caught in a double bind.

In regards to our actual findings, the students' reactions are explained more readily by the latter perspectives than by the structural perspective. Students in general rated the teaching of both men and women professors quite positively despite the differences in style. Specific style differences, however, affected the two sexes' competence and likability ratings differently, though not as predicted by the role conflict/status inconsistency argument. This perspective would argue that certain behaviors simultaneously increase likability ratings and lower competency ratings and vice versa. Yet the double bind reflected in this reasoning does not seem to be operating, at least not with respect to students' reactions. More often than not, a single given behavior on the part of women professors elicited a similar reaction (positive or negative) on both dimensions. For example, women professors were seen as both more likable and more competent the more they received solicited responses, generated laughter, gave partial negative evaluations, and acknowledged students' contributions. All of these behaviors are essential ingredients of the women's style as outlined above.

The same behaviors generally had no bearing (and sometimes had the opposite effect) on the evaluations of men professors. Apparently students appreciated the methods used by the women, but did not expect the same behaviors from male faculty. The only exception to this generalization is the pervasively positive effect of personalizations on the evaluations of both men and women. In this case, common expectations apparently existed for both sexes. One exception to this general rule, however, was that men were sanctioned negatively (by being judged as less competent) the more students personalized in their classrooms.

Women professors were expected to use the interactive model, and so were judged less likable the more they used classroom time to make presentations. (Men, on the other hand, were judged more likable for doing so.) Women, however, were expected to maintain control by using interactive methods (giving partial positive and negative feedback) and were sanctioned negatively for techniques that might signal lack of control (e.g., receiving many questions and solicitations from students). Thus, women were expected to walk a fine line, balancing the opportunity for students to participate with maintenance of a certain amount of control over the classroom; this situation also indicates a double bind. Even so, they did not seem to be faced with incongruous or contradictory expectations on the part of students by being simultaneously rewarded and punished for the same behaviors to the extent that the structural perspective would lead us to expect.

Judging by their evaluations, students appeared to expect conformity to the sex-differentiated teaching styles we observed among their professors. Men professors generally were evaluated more negatively the more they interacted with students and were evaluated more positively the more they held forth with presentations of material and managerial directives. Students evaluated their male professors positively when they gave negative corrective feedback and admonishments and when they interrupted students. In short, men were reinforced for maintaining their position of authority in the classroom, regardless of how they did so. Apparently the negotiation process had led to a general acceptance by students of these gender-differentiated teaching styles, in accordance with the interactionist and the contextual/woman-centered perspectives on roles and gender. Both approaches seemed to be equally effective.

Implications

Women's Position

On the whole, we find these results more consistent with the interactionist and the feminist perspectives on roles and gender than with the structural role conflict/status inconsistency perspective. Indeed, certain aspects of these findings—students' reactions, similarities in style, and effects of rank—can be accounted for only by the newer perspectives. Although writers recently have criticized the more traditional structural approach, few empirical tests such as this exist. It appears that men and women professors use different teaching styles in the university classroom, though these differences disappear under certain conditions and in regard to certain teaching issues. Such differences, presumably arising from cultural conditioning, also seem to be expected and reinforced by students. Although the professor's behaviors can be explained partially by the role conflict/status inconsistency argument, students' reactions generally cannot. In addition, the structural perspective cannot account for the lack of differences we found, whereas the other perspectives can.

We were intrigued when we saw how closely the approach of these women resembled the feminist pedagogy model set forth in related literature, whose major tenets include demystification of the research and teaching process, facilitation of innovation, and emphasis on the collaborative search for knowledge (Richardson, Fonow, and Cook 1985). Such epistemological intentions, together with commitment to personal and social change, mold the nature of what is taught, how it is communicated and received, and how the classroom is structured in terms of power exercised by students and professors. Strategies common to feminist pedagogy involve incorporating students' personal experiences as legitimate sources of insight through more experiential teaching techniques (Roth 1985) and placing students at the center of the learning process. Interestingly, the emphasis within feminist pedagogy on cooperative exchange of ideas and reactions to new insights contradicts directly the male-centered tendency to equate intelligence and authority with competitive, intellectual argumentation (Hall and Sandler 1982; Thorne 1979). The notion of feminist pedagogy and of its accompanying themes adds another dimension to our consideration of professorial teaching styles when we consider that little research has addressed the prevalence of such an approach. We do not know the extent to which feminist scholars themselves adhere to this philosophy, nor the prevalence of this orientation among women professors in general. Our findings confirm the existence of a "female mode" or a "woman's style" (either newly forming or reaffirmed) in matters of communication (see Stanley and Wolfe 1983 for further analysis).

Our findings suggest that many women professors are using elements of this feminist approach. Certainly their approach permits the reduction of differences in power (by involving students as partners in learning) and the working through of students' emotional responses (by encouraging personal contributions). Although many of these women do not describe themselves as feminists, these findings suggest that the feminist pedagogy model is rooted in general female experience. Additionally, some of these women may have been affected by the collaborative learning movement, which emphasizes cooperation among students and faculty in the classroom, an approach shown to enhance learning in diverse types of situations (Kurfiss 1987; Whipple 1987). Some of the same strategies, such as shared power in classroom process and course design, are seen in both the feminist pedagogy and collaborative learning literatures.

Whatever the sources of the techniques used by these women, they represent many strengths that might be incorporated into men's teaching styles as well, although the interviews suggest that students' expectations probably would have to change considerably before men would be comfortable in doing so.

These findings certainly negate the common belief that professional women are caught in situations where it is impossible for them to be effective. We find them to be functioning quite effectively. It is true, however, that women professors might encounter other types of difficulties, particularly with colleagues. Such difficulties are described in unreported data from our interviews and are well documented by Theodore's (1986) recent analysis.

Theoretical Integration

The puzzling aspect of our data was the fact that women assistants and associates reported a significant amount of conflict, even though their students' evaluations did not appear to represent a double bind for them in the manner we had predicted. In our search for the bind or binds underlying the women's expressed contradictions we came to understand the importance of the *relationship* in organizing the way in which women faculty members view the teaching aspect of their professorial roles. Here, the double bind was not articulated as simultaneously rewarding and punishing women for the same behavior (for example, reacting to personalizing techniques by "liking" the woman professor but seeing her as less "competent"), as was predicted by the structural version. Instead the bind centered around their students' expectations that they should behave in many stereotyped ways not demanded of men faculty members. At the same time, however, our evidence showed that women often were not behaving in these stereotyped ways; our interview materials showed that some women, especially senior faculty, resisted students' attempts to place them in maternal, emotionally manipulable roles. Here we see the operation of the process of role acquisition over time; students and teachers must reaffirm the old role definitions and their underlying cultural values even as they are working together to forge new definitions. Paradoxically, this situation places students and women professors in positions where they are simultaneously reinforcing and altering the structurally constraining definitions of gender and gender-appropriate behavior that each party brings to the situation.

The identification of this paradox arising from pressures to be a "real woman" appears to be a clearer perspective from which to understand the situation of women faculty; it takes into account their somewhat special cultural and social context within large universities. By contrasting it with the more structural prediction derived from role theory we can gain some insight into the point where the perspectives intersect. In its focus on *accommodation to* rather than *redefinition of* roles, the structural perspective posits a central premise: the best women can do is to contain or manage role conflict through the various techniques documented in research on this approach (such as Goode's (1960) classic statement on management strategies, including "compartmentalization," "barriers against intrusion," and "delegation of responsibility"). Instead, the implication of our research is that role obligations and rights will be altered in a way that accommodates both students and professors. Not having to alter expected role relationships in the first place would be the least stressful situation, which would promote the highest degree of role-person integration and more successful role performance. Thus, in the structural version of role theory the best women professors can hope for is to improve a difficult status position, with the underlying assumption that the initial disadvantage will mean poorer chances for successful evaluation by students (as reflected in the statement, "My prof isn't bad . . . for a woman.").

Instead the evidence shows that women can convince students to alter their expectations and to redefine how they can relate to college faculty and learn in the classroom. Thus, the question becomes, "What are the processes by which role partners come to define their role relationship and the need to alter it, and how do they coordinate these activities?"

Certainly power and authority are important here; they determine who has the final word and which actor can do the other the most harm. Viewed from a power/dependency perspective (Emmerson 1962), the individual with the least dependency will have the most power, so that professors—even women professors—typically are able to impose their will in a particular situation, given their relative power over students in the form of grades and ability to pass or fail a student in a course. In addition, a consideration of the more woman-identified forms of power such as "influence techniques" (Safilios-Rothschild 1970) and other less coercive change-oriented strategies (Ghiloni 1987b; Johnson 1976) suggests that women actually might be at an advantage relative to men in situations requiring negotiation, such as college classrooms. If we view the professorial role itself as creating a need for such skills in dealing with students, the focus shifts to women's ability to excel in managing these role relationships. In other words, incorporation of the interpretive framework shifts the focus away from structural limitations and toward the actor's agency in constructing his or her own role obligations and relationships.

The addition of the interpretive approach makes more fluid the ways in which we view the role relationship and definitions of rights and obligations. The context also is allowed to enter in here, so that we can account for different negotiation strategies in different settings and perhaps even for different types of role relationships between the same actors in these various contexts. The use of different strategies is exemplified by the women faculty members who preferred to avoid dealing directly (face-to-face) with students' grade challenges but were more likely than their male counterparts to be willing to listen to students' personal troubles. Another example includes women professors who are liked for giving partial corrective (negative) feedback and who always give the students at least some positive feedback as well. Examples of establishing different role relationships include the women students who were looking for female mentors to know personally and men students who wanted to establish "drinking buddy" or "racquetball partner" relationships with their male professors. This ability to recognize and account for flexibility in role portrayals is important if we are seeking context-sensitive understanding and is indispensable if we are taking a woman-centered perspective and wish to capture the unique tasks confronting women faculty members.

The dilemma we discovered for women professors points up an interesting paradox: although a woman might wish to retain some aspects of her "typical" female role and discard others, the ones she wishes to retain might put her at a disadvantage by emphasizing styles (cooperative, relationship-centered, affective, egalitarian) that conflict with the idealized competitive, status-driven, argumentative, individualistic academic environment (Van Der Berghe 1972). This conflict is different for the men faculty, who complain of too much distance between themselves and students. They have not taken on the "extra" activities of relationship building, even though many seem to be vaguely dissatisfied with the results of not doing so. They do not feel conflict between their occupational and their gender roles. Instead they are disconcerted by certain negative outcomes arising from both roles (and their accompanying statuses).

Perhaps we were wrong to look for the authority issue with women; perhaps women's focus on the twin goals of caring and connection made it inevitable that the central issue would be a matter of relationship building and how to balance this imperative with a vast array of professional demands. In other words, instead of leading us to the predicted double bind arising out of structural contradictions in the woman professor's position, the woman-centered, contextualized perspective brought us to an interpretive approach: we saw that the crucial issue for many respondents was the negotiation of role definitions that they and their students could accept and within which their students could learn.

Women's greater tendency to be concerned with caring, connectedness, and "who gets hurt," as discussed by Gilligan (1982), can be viewed as a mechanism for integrating the role conflict/status inconsistency argument with the interpretive perspective on roles. Both men and women faculty care whether their students learn, but they bring different skills to the learning enterprise which allow them to articulate their caring in different ways. Equally important, however, are the efforts that the women and their students often make to move toward new relationships, particularly when we keep in mind that not all women are equally at ease with the emphasis on caring/connectedness nor are they accustomed to employing it in a professional context. It is likely, however, that women with better interpersonal skills as well as impressive professional accomplishments will succeed in ascending the academic hierarchy.

Also, women's focus on relationships and on relating to students can be said to promote more effective learning. Attention to "relatedness" (e.g., relating information to one's own personal life, the ability to understand intuitively another person's point of view) is an especially effective way of teaching. Thus, in addition to possible advantages over men faculty in managing role relationships with students, women professors also might have an advantage in pedagogical implementation, especially if they believe firmly in the integrity of both teacher and student. Such professors regard teaching and learning as nonexclusive activities and view them as both means and ends rather than merely as means to an end (Schneidewind 1987). Of course, not all women are able to apply this caring/connectedness emphasis to their style of teaching, especially as it is articulated in students' expectations. Yet we have evidence that students reward their professors for behaviors that conform to sex-stereotypical expectations.

The notion of the relationship as a mechanism for synthesizing the normative and the interpretive frameworks is especially relevant to contexts undergoing change, as was (and is) the case at this large university in the 1980s and 1990s. Consequently this theoretical synthesis also might be useful in understanding other contexts undergoing transformation, such as the family, other work settings, and politics.

Our findings, then, have implications for the viability of role theory as a framework for studying gender differences. Interpretive role theory led us to expect students, as significant others, to play an important part in defining and enforcing role expectations. This expectation was upheld in several striking ways and confirmed a major tenet of interactive role theory, namely the role-taking process. Moreover, the importance of the relationship and concern with its quality and maintenance undergird the entire contextual approach that we found so useful in interpreting our data. Further studies such as this eventually might link gender research with the main body of social psychology, a goal that many feminists scholars hope to attain.

Several interlinked propositions emerged from our reflections on these findings. The first informs symbolic interactionism and structural role theory.

Proposition 1:   Master roles, such as gender, will influence the role negotiation process of most other roles enacted by individuals.

This proposition permeates our findings. The way in which ostensibly gender-neutral roles are enacted will vary greatly depending on the individual's gender. We have found variations by gender in the way in which the university professor role is played, as others have found for schoolteachers (Brophy and Good 1974; Good et al. 1973), managers (Leavitt and Lipman-Blumen 1980; Statham 1987), and members of other occupations. Stryker (1987) pointed to this proposition by arguing that master roles will come into play *only* in conjunction with the playing of other roles. Here we argue that they nearly always do so.

Of course we also find similarities, with rank an important factor in accounting for male-female convergence. Hence, the following hypothesis:

Proposition 1a: Master roles, such as gender, will influence the negotiated portrayal of other roles more heavily early in the life course of acquired roles and less heavily later in the life course of acquired roles.

This proposition is drawn chiefly from our findings about the effects of rank, a conveniently clear demarcation of the life course stages in the professor role. Rank is a strong factor, which mitigates gender differences. This pattern also might be explored for other roles, such as managers. Here, too, as women receive promotions and attain higher ranks, they might come to function more like their male peers. This pattern might exist for other master statuses as well.

Proposition 1b: Expectations of master roles, such as gender, will be incorporated more easily into the enactment of other roles when a power imbalance exists between role partners.

Certainly in this study, the fact that women had formal power and authority over their students facilitated their efforts at role negotiation. In situations where the power imbalance is not in their favor, these efforts might be less successful, as reported by Statham (1987) concerning the reactions of women managers' superiors to their managerial styles, or by Theodore (1986) concerning male peers' reactions to women professors.

Proposition 2:   A major goal in role negotiation is the development of a desired type of relationship between role partners.

The role theory literature has virtually ignored the quality of the relationship as an essential motivator in role negotiation and role playing. This factor can have tremendous implications for the way in which roles are enacted.

Proposition 2a: A gender difference often will exist concerning the type of relationship desired between role partners. Women more often will prefer a more personal, other-centered type of relationship, whereas men more often will prefer a more narrowly defined, utilitarian relationship.

Proposition 2b: The type of relationship formed between role partners will serve to further the accomplishment of the task inherent in the role relationship.

Rather than separating task functions from socioemotional functions of role portrayals, we argue that the two activities often are merged and carried out by the same individual, particularly by women. Thus, the utilitarian and the person-centered role relationships preferred respectively by men and by women are both aimed at task accomplishment.

Methodological Approaches

Our results also demonstrate the tremendous advantage of a triangulated approach to research, particularly one in which information is elicited from both partners in a role relationship. We were impressed continually by the extent to which the findings from our different methodologies informed and complemented one another, as others have contended (cf. Merton 1957; Whyte 1984). Our interview data provided depth and understanding to the interpretations we could give to all of our findings; our observation data, in turn, provided more generalizable evidence about actual behaviors and trends that our respondents discussed in the interviews. The students' evaluation data added yet another rich source of parallel information, against which to check professors' perceptions and by which to understand the students' points of view. Using both qualitative and quantitative approaches provided us with insights and knowledge that neither could have offered alone.

Such supposedly different epistemological assumptions, resulting in different data-gathering techniques, produced data that converged on a single, consistent social reality. This convergence—a mutually reinforcing and clarifying effect—speaks both to those who argue the superiority of quantitative approaches and to those who argue the inherent feminism or political correctness of qualitative approaches. If the aim of feminist research is to provide women with accurate descriptions of their situations, it behooves us to use any combination of methods necessary to preserve the complexity of the information, so that women can understand their situations more clearly and can make informed choices. Used together, the data provided powerful insights, whereas either approach used alone might have resulted in distortions or misunderstandings.

Triangulation enabled us to use findings from different methodological dimensions in order to see university teaching as a *system* of relationships, reported norms, actual behaviors, and emotional reactions. The discovery of inconsistencies between what respondents said and what they did led us to look for other inconsistencies in the data and to ponder their meaning; the uncovering of convergences in the different analyses led to greater confidence in certain underlying trends. This advanced level of analysis, in which findings from different schools are interrelated, is well suited for studying women, particularly professional women. In other examples of a triangulated approach, Kanter's (1977) research on men and women in a large multinational corporation used participant observation in meetings, interviews of new women sales managers, questionnaires completed by sales workers and by their managers, and company performance evaluations to understand women's experiences in corporate business settings. Similarly, Roberts' study of relationships between women and their doctors (1981) used content analysis of medical records, interviews with patients and with doctors, and content analysis of professional literature and medical journals to elucidate the gender politics of medicine.

Triangulation is an especially important strategy for studying women because it helps to fill information gaps stemming from the androcentrism of previous research in an area or topic (Cook 1983). Because the position of devalued groups is difficult to study in view of their "invisible" status and the complexity of many forms of oppression (Cook and Fonow 1986; Fishman 1978; Gardner 1980), triangulation is especially well suited for understanding women's experiences in a highly patriarchal institution such as academia (Cook and Fonow 1984). As such it enables the serendipitous discovery of findings that are less likely to emerge with use of only one method (Hacker 1980, 1981). It also enables us to incorporate new theoretical perspectives on gender as they are developed and articulated. Without multiple sources of insight, it would have been difficult to accomplish this type of integration.

Practical Applications of the Study's Findings

Implications for Professors

As far as university teaching is concerned, our results make two points. First, men and women use approaches that are different in many ways. Second, these approaches lead to equally desirable outcomes, at least so far as student evaluations are concerned. Thus, any efforts to impart knowledge about teaching itself must explore a range of techniques, including organizing lectures, effectively delivering material, involving students, generating more student participation of higher quality, and sharing power with students in the classroom. So, for example, our results indicate that the key to successful methods of sharing power are techniques that simultaneously reinforce the professors' subject matter authority. Attempts to impart effective teaching strategies must incorporate this delicate balance of power and authority with classroom openness.

While many academic departments have recently instituted programs to assist graduate students in becoming effective teachers, it is our impression that these efforts tend to be based upon the male model of teaching. For example, one of the authors attended a workshop directed by a highly respected leader in the field of teaching sociology. During the workshop this individual referred to the "mother hen" method of teaching, obviously viewing the methods we found most often used by women as irrelevant to the task of conveying the material. We hope that our findings will broaden the scope and diversity of teaching methods recognized as effective and as well received by students.

Our results indicate that many women professors experience a type of double bind, the result of managing discrepant statuses. Thus, they had to recognize the emotional stress generated by this bind and develop ways to deal effectively with it. Some of the women faculty we interviewed told us that they shared their reactions to their stress with other junior faculty, particularly other women assistant professors. Some women discussed their conflicts with senior faculty known to be sympathetic to students' needs; however, this strategy had the danger of backfiring negatively on the professors' chances of promotion if the senior member chose to share this knowledge with other members of the department. Other women professors talked with their spouses and partners, read "how to be a manager" books, or used physical exercise and meditation to manage teaching stress.

Our results also highlight the importance of learning to balance the sometimes overwhelming requirements of teaching along with other parts of an academic career such as community service, research, and publishing. At this university, the rewards for the latter two far exceeded the former two, and some women tended to get "bogged down" in becoming good teachers to the detriment of their ability to gain tenure and promotion. This was especially likely if the new teacher simultaneously was dealing with student challenges to her subject matter authority, often leading her to feel inadequate and to overemphasize students' reactions. Teachers need to recognize that some students' problems arise from the students themselves, and that faculty can only go so far in helping students with racism, sexism, homophobia, or other prejudices as they try to cope with the challenges of academic life.

Finally, faculty can benefit from recognizing how the presentation of self in the classroom influences professors' ability to manage authority and to create effective learning environments. Collaborative approaches to learning are indeed influenced by the manner in which students perceive and react to aspects such as dress, styles of speech, gestures, voice volume, and inflection. Men and women professors who ignore these aspects might encounter impediments in their efforts to establish satisfying relationships with students.

Implications for Administrators

College administrators must reconize that the needs of male and female professors might differ. For example, our results indicate that both sexes were judged equally competent when employing an evaluation instrument widely used at colleges and universities around the country the (SET). Possibly, other instruments currently in use contain measures of behaviors more typical of men (correcting students, offering their own opinions) or more typical of women (relating the class material to students' lives, personalizing from their own lives). In constructing evaluation instruments that measure specific behaviors, items tapping both types of behaviors ought to be included to avoid favoring one or the other approach. Also, items asking women and minorities about the climate they feel the professor created for participation, including any racial or sexual harassment, might well be included in faculty evaluations.

Faculty evaluations arise from two basic sources: colleagues as well as students. To assist senior colleagues in making fair and accurate assessments, administrators must help faculty re-examine their standards and indicators of good teaching. Just as new faculty (or graduate students) might not realize the range of effective teaching behaviors used by both men and women, senior faculty also might not appreciate women's approaches. Being organized and lecturing effectively might not be the pinnacle of good teaching. Time spent interacting with students inside and outside of the classroom seems to be just as important, but the tendency of men to regard these activities as "necessary time wastes" means that women's efforts might be systematically undervalued by their colleagues during evaluations for merit reviews or tenure and promotion.

We know of one administrator who insists that all faculty who evaluate the teaching of others in promotion decisions show evidence that they are aware of the new scholarship about teaching, particularly about women's approaches. It is the unfortunate result of the existing tenure system that women often are advised to spend less time with students and less effort on their teaching because they will not be rewarded and, in fact, might be punished if the energy expended means that they do less publishing. Administrators can provide the leadership necessary to overcome the detrimental effects of this philosophy on the quality of student instruction and faculty morale.

Because men and women tend to use different styles, negative implications of their teaching are also very different. Male faculty members, sanctioned by students for using interactive techniques, are often dissatisfied with the distance that exists between them and their students. Administrators seeking to encourage collaborative learning approaches among their faculty will need to help male professors work through their own and their students' reluctance to doing this. Encouragement to try collaborative techniques and share power in the learning enterprise also can be modeled for faculty by administrators in their *own* dealings with students and professors.

At the same time, women faculty experience the pressures of role conflict, particularly at the assistant and associate levels. They may also find themselves overburdened by too much contact with students, trying to manage student demands that they play a "mother" role in their approach to teaching. Also, their increased tendency to use personalizations is coupled with students' tendency to judge their personalities in their assessments of their performance. Hence, administrators might assist women in their efforts to resolve these many conflicts—and monitor the evaluation, tenure, and promotion system to see that extraneous factors are not entering in.

Our results also suggest that in-service training regarding interactive teaching styles and classroom management would be beneficial to all faculty. One type of challenging students, mentioned in our interviews, are those who threaten or coerce professors or other classmates; these students also require special approaches with which postsecondary faculty might have little experience. Managing the resistant, disruptive, or seductive student requires training needed by male as well as female faculty; in-service education in this area should be made available and its use encouraged by administrators. This training ought to incorporate the notion that men and women use different approaches in dealing with such students. Also, there is evidence that women's student-centered, relationship-focused teaching styles might be especially effective in teaching the more reticent, special needs student. Training in these styles may assist male professors to develop greater facility in dealing with challenging students.

Actually, today's modern university includes a wide array of students presenting many special challenges because of their diversity. This in-service training should offer approaches to all students with special needs (with whom many faculty have limited experience) such as returning students, minority students, gay and lesbian students, international students, women students, and students with physical and emotional disabilities.

Overall, administrators can benefit from the knowledge that university teaching is a complex phenomenon experienced differentially by men and women and by their students. Through developing better understanding of the gendered nature of this complexity, higher quality instruction and enhanced faculty development are made possible for both men and women professors.

Future Research

After conducting our study we have come to realize how future efforts might improve upon or expand the research design we used. One might conduct a similar study with repeated observations, using fewer variables. To generalize to college teaching in other contexts, it will be necessary to gather information at small universities and liberal arts colleges in regions other than the midwest. Patterns might differ in situations where attitudes toward women are more or less traditional than in the setting we studied. Looking across institutions also will enable the inclusion of more atypical women—specifically, women who are full professors and/or who teach in male-dominated departments as well as women of color. We know relatively little about such women because there were so few at this university.

We also suggest that different types of students' reactions be measured. In particular we would be interested in discovering whether differences in teaching style affect what students learn—or whether they affect students' perceptions of what they learn. Earlier research suggests that teaching styles have little to do with teachers' effectiveness or with how much students actually learn (Getzels and Guba 1954). Interviews with students, particularly those whose professors have been observed, would be an ideal way to capture more fully the interactive nature of this experience.

In sum, this study provides important insights into the situations of male and female professors in the university. Our findings that men and women used different, though apparently equally effective, approaches might be applied to the study of gender differences in other situations, particularly other professional settings. They also provide an impetus for examining professional socialization hypotheses with regard to different stages in a career (given our findings concerning rank) and to the existence of feminist pedagogy as an emergent phenomenon. We hope that our findings will prove helpful in easing the burdens felt either by women or by men as they attempt to manage their professional roles, if only by identifying a group experience with structural sources. To paraphrase C. Wright Mills, viable *and* liberating solutions can be found only by recognizing that whatever "personal problems" exist are also "social issues."

Appendices

Appendix A
The Hough-Duncan Observation Technique

This technique involves two basic categories: substantive and managerial. Substantive activity refers to behavior whose purpose is to teach the subject matter of the course; managerial behavior refers to behavior whose purpose is to facilitate the learning process. For each of these two basic categories there are twelve coded specific categories such as initiating, judging, and manipulating artifacts. Either students (code S) or teachers (code T) can engage in any of the two basic or the twelve specific categories and can have their behavior coded by the observer. For example, S–5 indicates a student responding to the professor about the class lesson, whereas T–5 indicates a teacher responding to a student's query about the lesson. The categories we use are the same as in the basic Hough and Duncan (no date) classification except that our specific category 2 refers to laughter, rather than their designation, "sensing" (see table A.1).

To distinguish even further between these behaviors in the classroom, we employed six subfunctions, which allowed us to code the contextual connotation of particular behaviors. Thus, for example, we can distinguish between laughter that ridicules and laughter that is supportive. In addition, we coded another set of modifying behaviors through the use of subscripts. Thus, for example, we could code students' challenges to professors, interruptions by either student or professor, and professors or students reviewing or summarizing material. Although Hough and Duncan regarded these codes as optional, we found them to be essential (see table A.2).

The measures, as constructed to tap the three aspects of teaching behaviors we considered, are presented in table A.3.

TABLE A.1
Modified Hough-Duncan Coding Categories

BASIC CATEGORIES		SPECIFIC CATEGORIES
Code Numbers		
Substantive	*Managerial*	*Specific Categories of Teachers' or Students' Behavior*
1	01	Think
2	02	Laugh
3	03	Manipulate artifacts
4	04	Initiate
5	05	Respond
6	06	Solicit clarification
7	07	Solicit
8		Judge correct
9		Personal positive judgment
10		Acknowledge
11		Judge incorrect
12		Personal negative judgment

SUBFUNCTIONS*
Code Letters

A	Accentuated/dramatic inflection (with substantive)
A	Admonishment (with managerial)
U	Unspoken
UM	Experiential
M	Personalization (may be subscripted "S" or "W"; otherwise applies to students when used with T behaviors)
AM	Ridicule
AUM	Implicitness

SUBSCRIPTS

C	Challenge to professor by student
B	Behavior specifically solicited by professor (not used with S5s)
J	Judgment of partial correctness
P	Positive reaction
N	Negative reaction
S	Self reference
W	"We" reference (with subfunctions M and AM)
I	Interrupting
O	Organizing, outlining, introducing
R	Review, summation, repetition
E	Explicit emphasis of particular points

*Any basic or specific category may be modified by one subfunction and/or one subscript.

TABLE A.2

Modified Hough-Duncan Expanded Definitions of Categories

Substantive behavior: Any manifest nonappraising behavior that is intended to facilitate the attainment of new learning, or to sustain or extinguish prior learning that is considered by those in the instructional situation to be a legitimate part of the subject matter of the field under study.

Managerial behavior: Any manifest, nonappraising, nonsubstantive behavior that is intended to create nonsubstantive conditions that facilitate the attainment of new learning or to sustain or extinguish prior learning.

1/01 *Thinking*: Any nonappraisal behavior in which a person is apparently reflecting on (thinking about) some substantive or managerial aspect of classroom instruction.

3/03 *Manipulating artifacts*: Any nonappraisal behavior in which one manipulates (works with) instructional artifacts (curricular-instructional materials).

4/04 *Initiating*: Any spoken, unspoken, or mediated nonappraisal behavior that presents substantive or managerial information to another or others. The initiating behavior may be an expression of knowledge and/or an expression of feeling states or value preferences.

5/05 *Responding*: Any spoken, unspoken, or mediated nonappraisal behavior that responds substantively or managerially to an element in the instructional situation . . . The responding behavior may be an expression of knowledge, a demonstration of a skill and/or an expression of a feeling state or value preference.

6/06 *Soliciting clarification*: Any manifest nonappraisal behavior . . . that evokes or is intended to evoke from another person the fuller meaning of an antecedent behavior of that person or a product of his or her behavior . . . The behavior intended to evoke the fuller meaning may be in the form of a question, direction, or suggestion.

7/07 *Soliciting*: Any manifest . . . nonappraisal behavior that evokes or is clearly intended to evoke substantive and/or managerial behavior from another person in the instructional situation. Specifically excluded here are those behaviors that fall in the category of soliciting clarification. For our purposes we adapted T07 to refer specifically to such behaviors as asking students if they had "any questions."

8 *Judging correctness*: Any manifest . . . behavior that responds or reacts to an antecedent behavior of the self or another or to a product of such

(Continued)

behavior . . . by judging the behavior or product . . . to have been logically, empirically, or normatively correct in some degree. Publicly accepted criteria are invoked or could be invoked to support the judgment.

9 *Personal positive judging*: Any manifest behavior . . . that responds or reacts to a person . . . , an antecedent behavior of the self or another, or to a product of such behavior . . . by expressing a personal, positive judgment about the person, behavior, or product of behavior. The criteria for making the judgment are personal . . .

10 *Acknowledging*: Any manifest . . . behavior that responds or reacts to a person . . . , to an antecedent behavior of the self or another, or to a product of such behavior . . . by acknowledging the person, behavior, or product in ways that indicate that the person, behavior, or product has been perceived. No judgment is explicitly expressed.

11 *Judging incorrectness*: Any manifest . . . behavior that responds or reacts to an antecedent behavior of the self or another or to a product of such behavior . . . by judging the behavior of the product . . . to have been logically, empirically, or normatively incorrect in some degree. Publicly accepted criteria are invoked or could be invoked to support the judgment.

12 *Personal negative judging*: Any manifest behavior . . . that responds or reacts to a person . . . , to an antecedent behavior . . . , or to a product of such behavior by expressing a personal negative judgment about the person, behavior, or product of behavior. The criteria for making the judgment are personal . . .

Subfunctions

A: Denotes talk accentuated by dramatic inflection that deviates from the speaker's normal style. With managerial behaviors, A indicates an admonishment.

U: Indicates an unspoken mode of communication, such as a nod or writing on the blackboard, that lasts for at least five seconds with no spoken behavior during the interval.

UM: Indicates in-class experiential activity used as an illustration of a course concept such as performing an experiment or working out a problem. Routine drills over homework are excluded.

(*Continued*)

M: Denotes a piece of talk in which the speaker is using personal information—i.e., about self or family—to convey or illustrate a point. When used with teacher's behaviors unsubscripted, the professor refers to the students' personal lives. References to the professor's life by the professor were subscripted S (see below).

AM: Denotes a piece of talk that ridicules another or others.

AUM: Denotes an implicit evaluation in a nonevaluative behavior (e.g., while initiating or responding).

Subscripts

C: Denotes a piece of students' talk that challenges the teacher by questioning a substantive point, the teacher's authority, or a source of information.

B: Indicates a student's behavior that is specifically solicited by the teacher but is not a verbal response to a question.

J: Indicates a nonappraisal behavior that involves a partial judgment.

P: Indicates a positive reaction involved in an implicit evaluation (used with subfunction AUM).

N: Indicates a negative reaction involved in an implicit evaluation (used with subfunction AUM).

S: Indicates that a statement contains an explicit reference to the speaker's self (used with subfunctions M and AM).

W: Indicates that a statement contains an explicit reference to the communal "we" (used with subfunctions A and AM). In case of admonishments, W refers to the group as a whole.

I: Indicates that a piece of talk has interrupted the previous speaker.

O: Indicates that talk is organizing what is to come, is ordering or outlining substance or process, or is prefatory.

R: Indicates that talk is giving information in a summary, review, or repeated form.

E: Indicates that a piece of talk is indicated explicitly as containing important information, i.e., it is given emphasis.

TABLE A.3

Measures of Teaching Behaviors

Presentation of Material

Structured presentation indicators
Managerial behaviors
Ordering presentations
Miscellaneous managerial behaviors

Minimal use of participatory learning model
Responses to students' questions
Professor's solicitations of clarification
Managerial solicitations

Extensive use of participatory learning model
Experiential activities
Soliciting students' input
Solicitations by students
Total students' input
Students presenting material
Professors'/students' thought
Professors'/students' laughter

Authority Management

Establishing legitimacy as authority
Positive feedback
Negative feedback
Unspoken positive feedback

Harshness of control techniques
Partial positive feedback
Ridicule
Admonishments
Interruptions by professors

Reducing appearance of authority
Challenges by students
Evaluative statements by students
Interruptions by students

Personalizations

Personalizations
General personalization
Professors' references to self
Professors' references to students
Students' personalizations
Professor acknowledging students
Professor empathizing with students

Appendix B
Observer Effects Estimated with ANOVA

To test for the possibility of observer effects, we performed analyses of variance (ANOVA) within the four-category breakdown of our sample (men and women in male-dominated and non-male-dominated departments). These equations used a four-category observer variable (there were four observers) to predict the proportion of time spent on specific behaviors as they were coded. (See table B.1.)

We examine "observer effects" only on basic and on specific categories of behavior because this is the most critical distinction to be made. These behaviors occurred most often; the unreported effects on the other behaviors did not differ substantially from these. In addition, these were the kinds of behaviors in which we expected the most consistency across observers; other less frequent behaviors (many of the subscript and subfunction behaviors) actually might have occurred less consistently across individuals.

Although there are some significant effects, they were scattered and very rare. Upon closer examination and in conversations with observers, we could trace most of these effects to one or two particular observations. For instance, one observer reported several cases where TO4 and T4 were difficult to distinguish because the professor used a style that mixed substantive and managerial behaviors throughout the lecture. In some cases, it was possible to modify the data. Even so, we do not believe that the differences among observers are sufficient to distort our findings seriously; indeed, we are struck by the high degree of agreement among them.

TABLE B.1

ANOVA "F" Probability Values Testing for Observer Effects (Teachers' Behaviors)

	Women	Men	Women	Men
	Nonmale-Dominated	Nonmale-Dominated	Male-Dominated	Male-Dominated
T4	.0351*	.2167	.5362	.6697
T5	.3630	.0323*	.4452	.7644
T6	.4979	.1991	.4682	.2614
T7	.5508	.0787	.9532	.3021
T8	.1595	.3213	.5008	.2861
T9	.2679	.0975	.1925	.3849
T10	.6903	.2893	.5817	.9552
**T11	.005*	.0156*	.1097	.2661
T12	.0581	.0093*	.6242	.1726
T03	.1683	.3566	.0098*	.2176
**T04	.0115*	.6793	.9649	.0450*
T05	.0986	.5965	.0992	.3054
T06	.0836	.0068*	.1479	.1817
T07	.5872	.6580	.8786	.5673
**S4	.0002*	.0192*	.2412	.2280
S5	.5813	.4275	.3594	.7617
S6	.3084	.3540	.0413*	.0711
S7	.7085	.4179	.3610	.6751
S8	.1208	.0490*	.3958	.2277
S9	—	.0257*	—	.5838
S10	.0000*	.1492	.0581	.3072
S11	.1374	.0067*	.2066	.5782
S12	.0549*	.2312	.2523	.2580

*p ≤ .05

**More than one category with significant observer effect.

Appendix C
The Construction of Student Evaluation Scales: Competence and Likability

We wanted to be sure that these items truly measured the two dimensions of competence and likability that they were intended to measure. An orthogonal factor analysis (table C.1) shows that to some extent this was true for the entire sample. Competence items tend to load more highly on factor 1 (several load on factor 3); and the likability items load more highly on factor 2. (Factor 3 was not significant, as indicated by an eigenvalue of less than 1, and so may be discounted.) This tendency becomes even stronger if we consider these items as they factor for male and female professors separately. For women professors (table C.2), these factors are more distinct, whereas for men professors (table C.3), some competence items appear only on the "affect" factor and some affect items appear only on the competence factor. Students apparently do not differentiate these two dimensions as carefully for men as for women professors; judgments of likability and of competence are not made quite as distinctly. Hence, in further analysis we constructed separate student evaluation scales for men and for women professors. The reliability of these scales were (1) .91 for the men's competence scale, which included items 1, 3, 4, 6, and 7; (2) .91 for the men's likability scale, which included items 2, 5, 10, and 11; (3) .96 for the women's competence scale, which included items 1, 2, 3, 4, 5, 6 and 11; and (4) .94 for the women's likability scale, which included items 7, 9, and 10. Notice that we deleted from all scales the item asking whether

TABLE C.1

Results from Orthogonal Factor Analysis for
Evaluation Items, Whole Sample

	Competence	Likability	Competence II
1. Teacher is prepared	.804	−.066	.249
2. Teacher has thorough knowledge	.142	.211	.868
3. Teacher communicates well	.923	.231	.175
4. Teacher is stimulating	.845	.366	.117
5. One of best teachers	.617	.433	.580
6. Teacher's presentations are logical	.883	.144	.163
7. Teacher is responsive to students	.229	.846	.361
8. Teacher is too authoritarian	.019	−.821	−.174
9. Teacher is considerate of students	.587	.665	−.197
10. Want to know teacher informally	.304	.702	.491
11. Best male/female teacher have had	.534	.539	.557
Eigenvalue			
Factor 1 6.601			
Factor 2 1.673			
Factor 3 0.927			

Note: Factor loadings of .30 or greater are considered to be significant; they are underlined.

the professor was "too authoritarian" (item 8); a reliability analysis suggested that the scales would be more reliable if this item was removed. On face value it seems to tap a slightly different area of concern, or it might have been a "red flag" to some students.

After we summed the items to form the scales, women's average scores were 13.812 for competence and 5.870 for likability. Men's average scores were 14.278 for competence and 8.633 for likability. Some of the differences exist because different numbers of items were used to form the two scales for each sex. The competence scale for women is composed of seven items; for men it is composed of five items. The likability scale for the women is composed of three items; while for men it is composed of four items.

TABLE C.2

Results from Orthogonal Factor Analysis for Evaluation Items,
Women Professors

	Competence	Likability
1. Teacher is prepared	.865	.037
2. Teacher has thorough knowledge	.854	.016
3. Teacher communicates well	.827	.460
4. Teacher is stimulating	.721	.623
5. One of best teachers	.852	.491
6. Teacher's presentations are logical	.808	.373
7. Teacher is responsive to students	.345	.869
8. Teacher is too authoritarian	.061	−.808
9. Teacher is considerate of students	.495	.880
10. Want to know teacher informally	.800	.739
11. Best male/female teacher have had	.534	.538
Eigenvalue		
Factor 1 7.559		
Factor 2 1.606		

Note: Factor loadings of .30 or greater are considered to be significant; they
are underlined.

TABLE C.3

Results from Orthogonal Factor Analysis for Evaluation Items,
Men Professors

	Competence	Likability
1. Teacher is prepared	.850	.006
2. Teacher has thorough knowledge	−.039	.771
3. Teacher communicates well	.950	.182
4. Teacher is stimulating	.888	.214
5. One of best teachers	.548	.713
6. Teacher's presentations are logical	.909	.097
7. Teacher is responsive to students	.192	.910
8. Teacher is too authoritarian	−.022	−.767
9. Teacher is considerate of students	.629	.243
10. Want to know teacher informally	.254	.903
11. Best male/female teacher have had	.433	.827
Eigenvalue		
Factor 1 5.945		
Factor 2 2.447		

Note: Factor loadings of .30 or greater are considered to be significant; they
are underlined.

APPENDIX D
Student Questionnaire and Interview Guide

QUESTIONNAIRE

1. Major: A) Social Sciences   D) Other
                       B) Natural Sciences   E) Undecided
                       C) Humanities and Arts
2. GPA: A) 3.5–4.0   D) 2.0–2.4
                       B) 3.0–3.4   E) Below 2.0
                       C) 2.5–2.9
3. Grade expected in this course: A) A   B) B   C) C   D) D   E) E
4. This course is: A) only a BER requirement for me B) required for my major C) part of my major but not required D) an elective
5. Sex: A) Female   B) Male
6. About how many college courses have you had where the major instructors were women?
                       A) none   D) 50 to 80%
                       B) 25% or less   E) practically all
                       C) 25% to 50%
7. About how many college courses have you had where the teaching assistants instructing were women?
                       A) none   D) 50 to 80%
                       B) 25% or less   E) practically all
                       C) 25% to 50%
8. Sex of Instructor: A) Female   B) Male

For each of the following statements blacken the letter which best expresses your opinion on each of the following items:

A	B	C	D	E
Strongly Agree	Agree	Neutral	Disagree	Strongly Disagree

9. The instructor was well prepared for class.
10. The instructor had a thorough knowledge of the subject.
11. The instructor communicated the subject matter well.
12. The instructor stimulated interest in the course subject.
13. The instructor is one of the best teachers I have known at this university.
14. The instructor presented the material in a logical manner.
15. This instructor was responsive to student input.
16. Sometimes, this instructor seems to be too authoritarian.
17. This instructor was generally very considerate of students.
18. If given the opportunity, I would like to know this instructor more informally.
19. Compared to most other female/male instructors, this one is among the best.
20. In general, I would rather be taught by male than female instructors.

INTERVIEW GUIDE

Code # _____
Sex _____
Department _____
Rank _____
Years of Teaching _____

Teaching Styles
I am interested in how females and males experience the teaching role in universities. I will be asking some general questions about your attitudes toward teaching and about your experiences with students in classrooms and in your office. I am particularly interested in the special insights and experiences you have had because you are a female (male). Although many of these questions are structured, please feel free to add areas and ideas which I may not be covering.

Attitudes
1. As you know, teaching is but one aspect of the professorial role. How would you characterize your present attitude towards teaching? (e.g., a chore, neutral, pleasurable, etc.)

2. Has your attitude toward teaching changed over the years you have been teaching? Become less/more pleasurable?

   2a. Source of change? (Probe: tenure, disenchantment, kinds of students, kinds of courses, lack of rewards, other interests, etc.)

3. How important is it to you personally at this time in your career to do an excellent job of teaching?

4. Has the importance of being excellent changed over the years? More/less?

   4a. Source of change? (Probe: other interests, tenure, no rewards, subject matter)

5. About how much time do you spend a week talking about your teaching? What sorts of things do you talk about?

6. Do you think you are about as good as, better than, or less good a teacher than your male/female colleagues at your rank?

7. Do you think your male/female colleagues are accurately evaluating your teaching ability?

8. When you have a teaching problem, how do you work it out? (Probe: Do you seek help from colleagues? Same-sex?)

9. Are there any other factors in your department that affect your teaching satisfaction and competence specifically because of your sex? (Probe: no same sex colleagues, competition amongst same sex, being put down, etc.)

Classroom

10. About how much time do you spend preparing for a class period?

11. Do you think you spend as much time/less time than your male/female colleagues at your rank?

12. How would you characterize your teaching style? (Open, informal, formal, discursive, experiential)

13. Would you give me an example of a particular classroom experience that you felt especially good about?

14. Would you give me an example of a particular classroom experience that you felt especially bad about?

15. Some professors report having management problems—e.g., students talking during lectures, reading newspapers, etc. Have you had these? How do you handle them?

16. Some professors report that students will challenge their competency and knowledge. Have you experienced that? How do you handle this?

17. Some professors report that students will ask personal questions about them in the classroom. Have you experienced that? How do you handle it?

18. Some professors report that students will make snide comments about them in the classroom. Have you experienced that? (Example?) How do you handle it?

19. Are there other things that go on in your classroom that you think are attributable to the fact that you are a woman (man)?

(Probe: Girls showing legs, students interrupting female speaker, etc.)

Student Evaluations
20. Do you think your students' evaluations fairly accurately reflect your competence as a teacher?

21. Do you ever get comments on your teaching evaluation forms which are not related to your competence as a teacher? (Probe: About your politics? Ideology? Personality? Clothing? Looks? etc.)

Office
22. Part of the teaching role, of course, involves seeing students outside of class in our offices. Currently, do you have a lot of students/a few/come to your office?

23. Have the numbers of students increased/decreased/remained about the same over the years you have been teaching?

23a. If changed, why do you suppose that is? (Probe: Prof. less open, students less interested, teaching different things, etc.)

24. Do you think more students come to your office than your male/female colleagues?

25. Do mostly male students or female students come or about half/half?

26. What approach(es) have male students used when they want a grade changed?

27. What approach(es) have female students used when they want a grade changed?

28. Do male students come to discuss things other than course work? If other things, how do you handle it?

29. Do female students come to discuss things other than course work? Such as? How do you handle it?

General

30. Are there other areas about your teaching that we haven't discussed that seem especially relevant?

31. Do you find you become friends with your students?

32. Do you find yourself in role conflict—role of women/role of professor?

33. Do students expect you to be a role model?

Notes

Chapter 1

1. Others emphasize collaborative learning, most notably those working in the collaborative learning movement. Here cooperative efforts among students, faculty, and administration are encouraged (Whipple 1987). Here, too, students share in the power in the classroom, working together in a cooperative manner, often helping to redesign the curriculum (Romer 1985; Whipple 1987). One difference between this approach and feminist pedagogy is the emphasis the first approach places on the notion that knowledge exists in the community, *not* with the individual, an idea that has not been well articulated by feminist pedagogists.

Chapter 3

1. We performed significance tests with regression equations predicting the proportion of time spent in each activity with variables measuring sex of professor (1=female), sex ratio of the professor's department (1=male-dominated; 0=nonmale-dominated), professor's rank, class size, and course level. Thus, all reported gender differences held true while we controlled simultaneously for the professor's departmental sex ratio, rank, class size, and course level. (See chapter 2 for a fuller explication.)

Chapter 4

1. We performed significance tests with regression equations predicting the proportion of time spent in each activity with variables measuring sex of professor (1=female) and controlling for sex ratio of professor's department (1=male-dominated; 0=nonmale-dominated), professor's rank, class size, and course level. (See chapter 2 for a fuller explication.)

Chapter 5

1. We performed significance tests with regression equations predicting the proportion of time spent in each activity with variables measuring sex of professor (1=female), controlling simultaneously for sex ratio of the professor's department (1=male-dominated; 0=nonmale-dominated), professor's rank, class size, and course level. (See chapter 2 for a fuller explication.)

Chapter 6

1. Zero-order correlations among control variables tended to be quite low, usually were not statistically significant, and in no case exceeded .50. Zero-order correlations between the control variables and the observation variables were also quite low; they never exceeded .40.

References

Ad Hoc Committee on the Education of Women at Oberlin. 1980. "The Education of Women at Oberlin." Office of the President, Oberlin College.

Addelson, Kathryn Pine. 1983. "The Man of Professional Wisdom: Cognitive Authority and the Growth of Knowledge." In *Discovering Reality: Feminist Perspectives on Epistemology, Metaphysics, Methodology, and Philosophy of Science*, edited by S. Harding and M. B. Hintikka. Boston: S. Reidel.

Adler, Emily Stier. 1984. "It Happened to Me: How Faculty Handle Student Reactions to Class Material." Working Paper No. 132, Wellesley College Center for Research on Women.

Aleamoni, Lawrence U., and Gary S. Thomas. 1980. "Differential Relationships of Student, Instructor, and Course Characteristics to General and Specific Items on a Course Evaluation Questionnaire." *Teaching of Psychology* 7:233–35.

Astin, Helen, and Alan Bayer. 1973. "Sex Discrimination in Academe." In *Academic Women on the Move*, edited by A. Rossi and A. Calderwood. New York: Russell Sage Foundation.

Auerbach, Judy, Linda Blum, Vicki Smith, and Christine Williams. 1985. "On Gilligan's: *In a Different Voice*." *Feminist Studies* 11:147–61.

Babladelis, Georgia. 1973. "Sex Stereotyping: Students' Perceptions of College Professors," *Perceptual and Motor Skills* 37:47–50.

Baker-Miller, Jean. 1982. "Women and Power." Colloquium, Work in Progress Series, Wellesley College, Wellesley, Mass.

Bandarage, Asoka. 1983. "From Universal Sexual Subordination to International Feminism: A Critical Assessment." Brandeis University. Mimeo.

Barndt, Deborah. 1980. *Education and Social Change: A Photographic Study of Peru*. New York: Kendall/Hunt.

Barnett, Linda Thurston, and Glenn Littlepage. 1979. "Course Preferences and Evaluations of Male and Female Professors by Male and Female Students," *Bulletin of the Psychonomic Society* 13: 44–46.

Basow, Susan A., and Nancy T. Silberg. 1985. "Student Evaluations of College Professors: Are Males Prejudiced against Women Professors?" Paper presented to the Eastern Psychological Association, Boston, Mass.

Bateson, G. 1960. "Minimal requirements of a theory of schizophrenia." *Archives of General Psychiatry* 2, 477–491.

Beard, Mary R. 1946. *Women as a Force in History: A Study in Traditions and Realities*. New York: MacMillan.

Belenky, Mary Field, Blythe McVicker Clinchy, Nancy Rule Goldberger, and Jill Mattuck Tarule. 1986. *Women's Ways of Knowing: The Development of Self, Voice, and Mind*. New York: Basic Books.

Bennett, William J. 1984. *To Reclaim a Legacy: A Report on the Humanities in Higher Education*. Washington, D.C.: National Endowment for the Humanities.

Benson, Donna, and Gregg Thomson. 1980. "Sexual Harassment on a University Campus: The Confluence of Authority Relations, Sexual Interest, and Gender Stratification." Paper presented at the annual meeting of the American Sociological Association, New York, New York.

Berheide, Catherine White, and Marcia Texler Segal. 1985. "Teaching Sex and Gender: A Decade of Experience." *Teaching Sociology* 12:267–84.

Bernard, Jessie. 1964. *Academic Women*. University Park: Pennsylvania State University Press.

Bloom, Alan. 1987. *The Closing of the American Mind: How Higher Education Has Failed Democracy and Impoverished the Souls of Today's Students*. New York: Simon and Schuster.

Blumer, Herbert. 1969. *Symbolic Interactionism: Perspective and Method*. Englewood Cliffs, NJ: Prentice-Hall.

Bridges, Amy, and Heidi Wartman. 1973. "Pedagogy by the Oppressed." *Review of Radical Political Economics* 6:75–79.

Bright, Clare. 1987. "Teaching Feminist Pedagogy: An Undergraduate Course." *Women's Studies Quarterly* 15:96–100.

Brophy, Jere E., and Thomas L. Good. 1974. *Teacher-Student Relationships: Causes and Consequences*, New York: Holt, Rinehart and Winston.

Broverman, I. K., D. M. Broverman, F. E. Clarkson, P. S. Rosenkrantz, and S. R. Nagel. 1970. "Sex-Role Stereotypes and Clinical Judgments of Mental Health." *Journal of Consulting and Clinical Psychology* 34:7–16.

Brown, Serena-Lynn, and Robert Klein. 1982. "Women-Power in the Medical

Hierarchy." *Journal of the American Medical Women's Association* 37:155-64.

Burchard, W. W. 1954. "Role Conflicts of Military Chaplains." *American Sociological Review* 19:528–35.

Campbell, Donald T., and Julian C. Stanley. 1963. *Experimental and Quasi-Experimental Designs for Research.* Boston: Houghton Mifflin.

Centra, John A. 1987. "Formative and Summative Evaluation: Parody or Paradox?" In *Techniques for Evaluating and Improving Instruction,* edited by J. Aleamoni. San Francisco: Jossey-Bass.

Check, John F. 1979. "Wanted! A Humorous Teacher." *The Physical Educator* 36:119–22.

Chow, Esther Ngan-Ling. 1985. "Teaching Sex and Gender in Sociology: Incorporating the Perspective of Women of Color." *Teaching Sociology* 12:299–312.

Cicourel, Aaron V. 1970. "Basic and Normative Rules in the Negotiation of Status and Role." *Recent Sociology, No. 2: Patterns of Communicative Behavior.* New York: MacMillian.

Cook, Judith A. 1983. "An Interdisciplinary Look at Feminist Methodology: Ideas and Practice in Three Academic Disciplines." *Humboldt Journal of Social Relations* 10(2):127–52.

————. 1984. "Influence of Gender on the Problems of Parents of Fatally Ill Children." *Journal of Psychosocial Oncology* 2:71–91.

————. 1988. "Who 'Mothers' the Chronically Mentally Ill?" *Family Relations* 37:1–14.

Cook, Judith A., and Mary Margaret Fonow. 1984. "Am I My Sister's Gatekeeper?: Cautionary Tales from the Academic Hierarchy." *Humanity and Society* 8:442–52.

————. 1986. "Knowledge and Women's Interests: Issues of Epistemology and Methodology in Feminist Sociological Research." *Sociological Inquiry* 56(1):2–29.

Daniels, Arlene Kaplan. 1967. "The low-caste stranger in social research." In *Ethics, Politics, and Social Research,* pp. 267–296, edited by G. Sjoberg. Cambridge: Schenkman.

Denzin, Norman K. 1978. *The Research Act,* 2nd ed. New York: McGraw Hill.

Douglas, Jack. 1970. "Understanding Everyday Life." In *Understanding Everyday Life,* edited by J. Douglas, pp. 3–44. Chicago: Aldine.

Dubois, Betty Lou, and Isabel Crouch. 1977. "The Question of Tag Questions in Women's Speech: They Don't Really Use More of Them, Do They?" *Language in Society* 4:289–94.

Duncan, Michael J., and Bruce J. Biddle. 1974. *The Study of Teaching*, New York: Holt, Rinehart and Winston.

Dunn, Kathleen. 1987. "Feminist Teaching: Who Are Your Students?" *Women's Studies Quarterly* 15:40–46.

Eichler, Margrit. 1980. *The Double Standard: A Feminist Critique of Feminist Social Science*. New York: St. Martin's Press.

Eisenstein, Hester. 1983. *Contemporary Feminist Thought*. Boston, Mass.: G. K. Hall & Co.

Elmore, Patricia, and Karen LaPointe. 1975. "Effect of Teacher Sex, Student Sex, and Teacher Warmth on the Evaluation of College Instructors." *Journal of Educational Psychology* 67:368–74.

Emerson, R. M. 1962. "Power-dependence relations." *American Sociological Review* 27:31–42.

Epstein, Cynthia. 1970. *Women's Place: Options and Limits in Professional Careers*. Berkeley: University of California Press.

Eskilson, Arlene, and Mary Glenn Wiley. 1974 *The Study of Teaching*. New York: Holt, Rinehart and Winston.

———. 1976. "Sex Composition and Leadership in Small Groups." *Sociometry* 39:183–93.

Esp, B. 1978. "Campus prisoners of stereotype." *Psychology Today*, November, 12–13.

Ferber, Marianne, and Joan Althaus Huber. 1973. "Sex of Student and Instructor: A Study of Student Bias." *American Journal of Sociology* 80:949–63.

Fidell, I. 1970. "Empirical Verification of Sex Discrimination in Hiring Practices in Psychology." *American Psychologist* 25:1094–98.

Fisher, Bernice. 1982. "Professing Feminism: Feminist Academics and the Women's Movement." *Psychology of Women Quarterly* 7:55–69.

———. 1987. "The Heart Has Its Reasons: Feeling, Thinking, and Community-Building in Feminist Education." *Women's Studies Quarterly* 15:47–58.

Fisher, Jerilyn. 1987. "Returning Women in the Feminist Classroom." *Women's Studies Quarterly* 15:90–95.

Fishman, Pamela M. 1978. "Interaction: The Work Women Do." *Social Problems* 25:397–406.

Follman, John. 1975. "Student Ratings of Faculty Teaching Effectiveness: Rater or Ratee Characteristics." *Research in Higher Education* 3:155–67.

Franklin, Phyllis. 1981. *Sexual and Gender Harassment in the Academy: A Guide for Faculty, Students, and Administrators*. New York: Commission on the Status of Women in the Profession, The Modern Language Association of America.

Frazier, Charles E. 1978. "The Use of Life-Histories in Testing Theories of Criminal Behavior: Toward Revising a Method," *Qualitative Sociology* 1:122–39.

Frazier, Nancy, and Myra Sadker. 1973. *Sexism in School and Society*. New York: Harper and Row.

Freedman, Susan Stanford. 1985. "Authority in a Feminist Classroom: A Contradiction in Terms?" In *Gendered Subjects: The Dynamics of Feminist Teaching*, edited by Margo Culley and Catherine Portuges. Boston: Routledge and Kegan Paul.

Freire, Paulo. 1970. *The Pedagogy of the Oppressed*. New York: Continuum.

Gardner, C. B. 1980. "Passing By: Street Remarks and the Urban Female." *Sociological Inquiry* 50:328–56.

Garfinkel, Harold. 1972. "Common Sense Knowledge of Social Structures: The Documentary Method of Interpretation." In *Symbolic Interaction: A Reader in Social Psychology*, edited by J. Manis and B. Meltzer. Boston: Allyn and Bacon.

Gerson, Judith. 1985. "The Significance of Gender as a Social Category." Paper presented to the American Sociological Association, Washington, D.C.

Gerson, Judith M., and Kathy Peiss. 1985. "Reconceptualizing Gender Relations." *Social Problems* 32:317–31.

Getzels, J. W., and E. G. Guba. 1954. "Role, Role Conflict and Effectiveness: An Empirical Study." *American Sociological Review* 19:164-75.

Ghiloni, Beth W. 1987a. "The Velvet Ghetto: Women, Power, and the Corporation." In *Power Elites and Organizations*, edited by G. William Domhoff and Thomas R. Dye. Beverly Hills, CA: Sage Publications.

―――. 1987b. "Power through the Eyes of Women." Paper presented at the annual meetings of the American Sociological Association. Chicago, IL, August 1987.

Gilligan, Carol. 1982. *In A Different Voice*. Cambridge, Mass.: Harvard University Press.

———. 1986. "Reply by Carol Gilligan." *Signs* 11:324–33.

Glaser, Barney G., and Anselm L. Strauss. 1967. *The Discovery of Grounded Theory: Strategies for Qualitative Research*. Chicago: Aldine Publishing Company.

Goffman, Erving W. 1957. "Status Consistency and Preference for Change in Power Distribution." *American Sociological Review* 22:275–88.

Goldberg, Peter. 1968. "Are Women Prejudiced Against Women?" *Transaction* 5:28–30.

Good, Thomas L., J. Neville Siber, and Jere E. Brophy. 1973. "Effects of Teacher Sex and Student Sex on Classroom Interaction." *Journal of Educational Psychology* 65:74–87.

Goode, William J. 1960. "A Theory of Role Strains." *American Sociological Review* 25:483–96.

Gordon, Suzanne. 1985. "Anger, Power, and Women's Sense of Self." *Ms.* 12:42–44, 112.

Graham, Patricia Albjerg. 1978. "Expansion and Exclusion: A History of Women in American Higher Education." *Signs* 3:759–73.

Grant, Linda. 1983. "Peer Expectations about Outstanding Competencies of Men and Women Medical Students." *Sociology of Health and Illness* 5:42–61.

Gray, Janet Dreyfus. 1983. "The Married Professional Woman: An Examination of Her Role Conflicts and Coping Strategies." *Psychology of Women Quarterly* 7:235–43.

Greeno, Catherine G., and Eleanor E. Maccoby. 1986. "How Different is the 'Different Voice'?" *Signs* 11:310–16.

Griffin, J. 1972. "Influence Strategies: Theory and Research. A Study of Teacher Behavior." Ph.D. dissertation, University of Missouri at Columbia.

Gross, Neal, W. S. Mason, and A. W. McEachern. 1966. *Explorations in Role Analysis: Studies of the School Superintendency Role*. New York: John Wiley and Sons.

Hacker, Sally. 1980. "Technological Change and Women's Role in Agribusiness." *Human Services in the Rural Environment* 5(1):6–14.

———. 1981 "The Culture of Engineering: Women, Workplace, and Machine." *Women's Studies International Quarterly* 4:341–53.

Hall, Roberta M., and Bernice Sandler. 1982. "The Classroom Climate: A Chilly One for Women?" Washington, D.C.: Project on the Status and Education of Women, Association of American Colleges.

Hartley, Ruth E. 1969. "Sex-Role Pressures and the Socialization of the Male Child." *Psychological Reports* 5:457–68.

Hesselbart, Susan. 1978. "Sex Role and Occupational Stereotypes: Three Studies of Impression Formation." *Sex Roles: A Journal of Research* 4:409-22.

Hewitt, J. P., and R. Stokes. 1975. "Disclaimers." *American Sociological Review* 40:1–11.

Hirsch, E. D., Jr. 1987. *Cultural Literacy: What Every American Needs to Know.* Boston: Houghton Mifflin.

Hodge, Robert W., Paul M. Siegel, and Peter H. Rossi. 1964. "Occupational Prestige in the United States, 1925–1963." *American Journal of Sociology* 70:290–93.

Hough, John, and James Duncan. No date. "The Hough-Duncan Method for Coding Classroom Interaction." Department of Education, The Ohio State University, Columbus.

Huber, Joan. 1973. "From Sugar and Spice to Professor." In *Academic Women on the Move,* edited by A. Rossi and A. Calderwood . New York: Russell Sage Foundation.

Jackson, Elton F. 1962. "Status Consistency and Symptoms of Stress." *American Sociological Review* 27:469–80.

Jick, Todd D. 1983. "Mixing Qualitative and Quantitative Methods: Triangulation in Action." In *Qualitative Methodology,* edited by John Van Maanen, 135–48. Beverly Hills, CA: Sage Publications.

Johnson, Janet. 1980. "Questions and Role Responsibility in Four Professional Meetings." *Anthropological Linguistics* 22:66–76.

Johnson, Paula. 1976. "Women and Power: Toward a Theory of Effectiveness." *Journal of Social Issues* 32:99–110.

Kanter, Rosabeth Moss. 1977. *Men and Women of the Corporation.* New York: Basic Books, Inc.

Karp, David A., and Williams C. Yoels. 1976. "The College Classroom: Some Observations on the Meanings of Student Participation." *Sociology and Social Research* 60:421–39.

Kaschack, Ellyn. 1978. "Sex Bias in Student Evaluations of College Professors." *Psychology of Women Quarterly* 2:235–43.

Kaufman, Debra, and Michael Fetters. 1980. "Work Motivation and Job Values among Professional Men and Women: A New Accounting." *Journal of Vocational Behavior* 17:251–62.

Kerber, Linda K. 1986. "Some Cautionary Words for Historians." *Signs* 11:304–10.

Kohlberg, Lawrence. 1963. "The Development of Children's Orientations towards a Moral Order: Sequence in the Development of Human Thought." *Vita Humana* 6:11–33.

Komarovsky, Mira. 1946. "Cultural Contradictions and Sex Roles." *American Journal of Sociology* 52:182–89.

Kulik, James A., and Chen-lin C. Kulik. 1974. "Student Ratings of Instruction." *Teaching of Psychology* 1:51–57.

Kurfiss, Joanne. 1987. "The Reasoning-Centered Classroom: Approaches that Work." *American Association for Higher Education Bulletin* 39:12–14.

Lakoff, Robin. 1975. *Language and Woman's Place.* New York: Harper and Row.

Lamberth, John, and Debra Kosteski. 1981. "Student Evaluations: An Assessment of Validity." *Teaching of Psychology* 8:8–11.

Langland, Elizabeth, and Walter Gove. 1981. *A Feminist Perspective in the Academy: The Difference It Makes.* Chicago: University of Chicago Press.

Lapadat, Judy, and Maureen Sessahia. 1977. "Male versus Female Codes in Formal Contexts." *Sociolinguistics Newsletter* 8:7–81.

LaRussa, Georgia Williams. 1977. "Portia's Decision: Women's Motives for Studying Law and Their Later Career Satisfaction as Attorneys." *Psychology of Women* 1:350–64.

Leavitt, Harold J., and Jean Lipman-Blumen. 1980. "A Case for the Relational Manager." *Organizational Dynamics* (Summer): 27–41.

Lee, Patrick. 1973. "Male and Female Teachers in Elementary Schools: An Ecological Analysis." *Teachers College Record* 75:79–88.

Lee, Patrick C., and Annie Lucan Wolinsky. 1973. "Male Teachers of Young Children: A Preliminary Empirical Study." *Young Children* 28:342–53.

Lenski, Gerard E. 1954. "Status Crystallization: A Non-Vertical Dimension of Status." *American Sociological Review* 19:405–13.

Lewis, Michael. 1972. "Parents and Children's Sex-Role Development." *School Review* 80:229–40.

Lipman-Blumen, Jean. 1984. *Gender, Roles, and Power*. Englewood Cliffs, N.J.: Prentice-Hall.

Lunneberg, Patricia. 1982. "Role Model Influences of Nontraditional Professional Women." *Journal of Vocational Behavior* 20:276–81.

Luria, Zella. 1986. "A Methodological Critique." *Signs* 11:316–21.

Mackie, Marlene. 1977. "Professional Women's Collegial Relations and Productivity: Female Sociologists' Journal Publications, 1967 and 1973." *Social Science Research* 61:277–92.

Maher, Frances. 1985a. "Pedagogies for the Gender-Balanced Classroom." *Journal of Higher Education* 65:48–64.

———. 1985 "Classroom Pedagogy and The New Scholarship on Women." In *Gendered Subjects: The Dynamics of Feminist Teaching*, edited by Margo Culley and Catherine Portuges. Boston: Routledge and Kegan Paul.

Marsh, Herbert. 1984. "Students' Evaluations of University Teaching: Dimensionality, Reliability, Validity, Potential Biases, and Utility." *Journal of Educational Psychology* 76:707–54.

Martin, Elaine. 1984. "Power and Authority in the Classroom: Sexist Stereotypes in Teaching Evaluations." *Signs* 9:482–92.

McGrath, Ellen, and Carl Zimet. 1977. "Similarities and Predictors of Speciality Interest among Female Medical Students." *Journal of the American Medical Women's Association* 32:361–73.

McKeachie, W. J. 1986. *Teaching Tips: A Guidebook for the Beginning College Teacher*. Lexington, MA: Heath Publishers.

———. 1987 "Can Evaluating Instruction Improve Teaching?" *Techniques for Evaluating and Improving Instruction*. San Francisco: Jossey-Boss.

McKee, John P. 1959. "Man's and Woman's Beliefs, Ideals and Self-Concepts." *American Journal of Sociology* 54:346–63.

Meeker, B. F., and P. A. Weitzel-O'Neill. 1977. "Sex Roles and Interpersonal Behavior in Task-Oriented Groups." *American Sociological Review* 42:91-105.

Merton, Robert K. 1957. "On Manifest and Latent Functions." In *Social Theory and Social Structure*, edited by R. Merton. New York: Free Press.

Merton, Robert K., and Elinor Barber. 1963. "Sociological Ambivalence." In *Sociological Theory, Values, and Socio-Culture Change*, edited by Edward A. Tiryakian. New York: Free Press.

Messer-Davidow, Ellen. 1985. "Knowers, Knowing, Knowledge: Feminist Theory and Education." *Journal of Higher Education*,65:8–24.

Miller, J., S. Lakovitz, and L. Fry. 1975. "Inequities in the Organizational Experiences of Women and Men." *Social Forces* 54:365–81.

Millman, Marcia, and Rosabeth Moss Kanter. 1975. "Editorial Introduction." In *Another Voice*, edited by Marcia Millman and Rosabeth Moss Kanter. New York: Anchor Books.

Mischel, H. 1974. "Sex Bias in the Evaluation of Professional Achievements." *Journal of Educational Psychology* 66:157–66.

Moore, Carol Ann. 1977. "Teaching Behavior Related to Teacher Cognitive Style and Sex." Paper presented to the American Educational Research Association, New York.

Noonan, John F. 1980. "White Faculty and Black Students: Examining Assumptions and Practices." Unpublished paper, Center for Improving Teaching Effectiveness, Virginia Commonwealth University, Richmond.

O'Barr, William M. 1984. "Asking the Right Questions about Language and Power." In *Language and Power*, edited by Cheris Kramarae, Mariel Schulz, and William M. O'Barr, pp. 260–280. Beverly Hills, CA: Sage Publications.

Omolade, Barbara. 1987. "A Black Feminist Pedagogy." *Women's Studies Quarterly* 15:32–39.

On Campus. 1977. "What Makes a Teacher Great?" The Ohio State University, October 6.

Parelius, Ann P. 1975. "Emerging Sex-Role Attitudes, Expectations, and Strains among College Women." *Journal of Marriage and the Family* 37:146-53.

Peck, Teresa. 1978. "When Women Evaluate Women, Nothing Succeeds like Success: The Differential Effects of Status upon Evaluations of Male and Female Professional Ability." *Sex Roles* 4:205–13.

Perry, Raymond, Philip Abrams, and Les Leventhal. 1979. "Educational Seduction: The Effect of Instructor Expressiveness and Lecture Content on Student Ratings and Achievement." *Journal of Educational Psychology* 71:107–16.

Pfohl, Stephen J. 1975. "Social Role Analysis: An Ethnomethodological Critique." *Sociology and Social Research* 59:243–65.

Pheterson, Gail, Sara B. Kiesler, and Philip Goldberg. 1971. "Evaluation of the Performance of Women as a Function of their Sex, Achievement, and Personal History." *Journal of Personality and Social Psychology* 19:144-48.

Pines, Ayola, and Ditsa Kafry. 1981. "Tedium in the Life and Work of Professional Women as Compared with Men." *Sex Roles* 7:963–77.

Richardson, Laurel. 1985. *The New Other Woman: Contemporary Single Women in Affairs with Married Men*. New York: Free Press.

Richardson, Laurel, Mary Margaret Fonow, and Judith Cook. 1985. "From Gender Seminar to Gender Community." *Teaching Sociology* 12:303–24.

Richardson, Laurel, and Verta Taylor. 1986. "Not Telling about One's Sexuality: Feminist Issues." Unpublished paper, Department of Sociology, Ohio State University, Columbus.

Richardson, Mary Sue. 1982. "Sources of Tension in Teaching Psychology of Women." *Psychology of Women Quarterly* 7:45–53.

Roberts, Helen. 1981. "Women and Their Doctors: Power and Powerlessness in the Research Process." In *Doing Feminist Research*, edited by H. Roberts. London: Routledge and Kegan Paul.

Roby, Pamela. 1973. "Institutional Barriers to Women Students in Higher Education." In *Academic Women on the Move*, edited by A. Rossi and A. Calderwood. New York: Russell Sage Foundation.

Romer, Karen. 1985. *Models of Collaboration in Undergraduate Education*. Providence, R.I.: Brown University.

Rosen, C. Bernard, and Carol S. Aneshensel. 1976. "The Chameleon Syndrome: A Social Psychological Dimension of the Female Sex Role." *Journal of Marriage and the Family* 38:605–17.

Rosenberg, Rosalind. 1982. *Beyond Separate Spheres: Intellectual Roots of Modern Feminism*. New Haven: Yale University Press.

Rosenshine, Barak. 1971. *Teaching Behaviors and Student Achievement*. Great Britain: National Foundation for Educational Research in England and Wales.

Rosenshine, Barak, and Norma Furst. 1973. "The Use of Direct Observation to Study Teaching." In *Second Handbook of Research on Teaching*, edited by Robert M. Travers. Chicago: Rand McNally and Company.

Rossi, Alice. 1968. "Women in Science: Why So Few?" *Science* 148:1196–202.

Rossi, Alice, and Ann Calderwood. 1973. *Academic Women on the Move*. New York: Russell Sage Foundation.

Roth, Robin L. 1985. "Learning about Gender through Writing: Student Journals in the Undergraduate Classroom." *Teaching Sociology* 12:325–38.

Rubin, Lillian. 1983. *Intimate Strangers*. New York: Harper and Row.

Russo, Mary, Richard Closson, James McKenney, Michael Spino, Ronald Stewart, Jake Thiessen, and Elaine Waller. 1983. "Collaborative Teaching and Research Between Basic and Clinical Sciences: Exploitation of the Barriers to Collaboration and Suggested Approaches to Achieve Collaboration." *American Journal of Pharmaceutical Education* 47:58–116.

Safilios-Rothschild, Constantina. 1970. "The Study of Family Power Structure: A Review 1960–1969." *Journal of Marriage and the Family* 32:539–52.

Schniedewind, Nancy. 1985. "Cooperatively Structured Learning: Implications for Feminist Pedagogy." *Journal of Higher Education* 65:74–87.

_____. 1987 "Teaching Feminist Process." *Women's Studies Quarterly* 15:15–31.

Schuster, Marilyn R., and Susan R. Van Dyne. 1985. "The Changing Classroom." In *Women's Place in the Academy: Transforming the Liberal Arts Curriculum*, edited by Marilyn R. Schuster and Susan R. Van Dyne. Totowa, N.J.: Rowman and Allanheid.

Schutz, Alfred, and Thomas Luckman. 1973. *The Structures of the Life World*. Evanston: Northwestern University Press.

Schwartz, Pepper, and Janet Lever. 1973. "Women in the Male World of Higher Education." In *Academic Women on the Move*, edited by A. Rossi and A. Calderwood. New York: Russell Sage Foundation.

Sherriffs, A. C., and R. F. Farrett. 1953. "Sex Differences in Attitudes About Sex Differences." *Journal of Psychology* 35:161–68.

Shor, Ira. 1980. *Critical Teaching and Everyday Life*. Boston: South End Press.

Shrewsberry, Carolyn. 1987. "What Is Feminist Pedagogy?" *Women's Studies Quarterly*,15:6–14.

Simpson, Adelaide. 1979. "A Perspective on the Learning Experiences of Black Students at VCU." Unpublished paper, Center for Improving Teaching Effectiveness, Virginia Commonwealth University, Richmond.

Smith, Dorothy. 1974. "Women's Perspective as a Radical Critique of Sociology." *Sociological Inquiry* 44(1):7–13.

_____. 1979. "A Sociology for Women." In *The Prism of Sex*, edited by Julia A. Sherman and Evelyn Torton Beck. Madison, Wis.: University of Wisconsin Press.

Stacey, Judith, and Barrie Thorne. 1985. "The Missing Feminist Revolution in Sociology." *Social Problems* 32:301–16.

Stack, Carol B. 1986. "The Culture of Gender: Women and Men of Color." *Signs* 11:321–24.

Stanley, Julia Penelope, and Susan J. Wolfe. 1983. "Consciousness as Style: Style as Aesthetic." In *Language, Gender, and Society*, edited by B. Thorne, C. Kramarae, and N. Henley. Rowley, MA: Newberry House.

Stanley, Liz, and Sue Wise. 1983. *Breaking Out: Feminist Consciousness and Feminist Research*. Boston: Routledge and Kegan Paul.

Statham, Anne. 1987. "The Gender Model Revisited: Differences in the Management Styles of Men and Women." *Sex Roles* 16: 409–29.

Sternglanz, Sarah Hall. 1979. "Sex Differences in Student-Teacher Classroom Interactions." Paper presented to the Research Conference on Educational Environments and the Undergraduate Woman, Wellesley, September.

Stokes, R. and J. P. Hewitt. 1976. "Aligning Actions." *American Sociological Review* 41:838–49.

Stryker, Sheldon. 1959. "Symbolic Interaction as an Approach to Family Research." *Marriage and Family Living* 11:111–19.

_____. 1980 *Symbolic Interactionism*. Menlo Park: Benjamin/Cummings.

_____. 1987. "Identity Theory: Developments and Extensions." In *Self and Identity: Psychosocial Perspectives*, edited by K. Yardley and T. Haness, 89–103. New York: John Wiley and Sons.

Stryker, Sheldon, and Anne Statham Macke. 1978. "Status Inconsistency and Role Conflict." *Annual Review of Sociology*.

Stryker, Sheldon, and Anne Statham. 1985. "Symbolic Interaction and Role Theory." In *The Handbook of Social Psychology*, 3rd ed., edited by Gardner Lindzey and Elliot Aronsen, 311–78. New York: Random House.

Swoboda, Marian J., and Jane Vanderbosch. 1984. "The Politics of Difference." *Journal of Educational Equity and Leadership* 4:137–47.

Theodore, Athena. 1986. *The Campus Troublemaker: Academic Women in Protest*. Houston: Cap & Gown Press.

Thomas, E. J., and B. J. Biddle. 1966. *Role Theory: Concepts and Research*. New York: John Wiley.

Thompson, Martha E. 1987. "Diversity in the Classroom: Creating Opportunities for Learning Feminist Theory." *Women's Studies Quarterly* 15:81–89.

Thorne, Barrie. 1979. "Claiming Verbal Space: Women, Speech and Language in College Classrooms." Paper presented at the Research Conference on Educational Environments and the Undergraduate Woman, Wellesley College, September.

———. 1983 "Rethinking the Way We Teach." In *Feminist Pedagogy and The Learning Climate*, edited by K. Loring. Proceedings of the Ninth Annual Great Lakes Colleges Association of Women's Studies Conference.

Thorne, Barrie, Cheris Kramarae, and Nancy Henley. 1983. *Language, Gender, and Society*. London: Newberry House.

Thorne, Barrie, and Zella Luria. 1986. "Sexuality and Gender in Children's Daily Worlds." *Social Problems* 33:176–90.

Thorne, Barrie, V. Powell, Beverly Purrington, R. Reasley, and C. Wharton. 1984. "Teaching Sociology of Sex and Gender." *Teaching Newsletter*, 4:2–7.

Thornton, Russell, and Peter M. Nardi. 1975. "The Dynamics of Role Acquisition." *American Journal of Sociology* 80:870–85.

Till, Frank J. 1980. "Sexual Harassment: A Report on the Sexual Harassment of Students." Washington, D.C.: National Advisory Council on Women's Educational Programs.

Tresemer, David. 1975. "Assumptions Made About Gender Roles." In *Another Voice*, edited by M. Millman and R. Kanter. Garden City: Anchor Books.

Turner, Ralph H. 1962 "Role-Taking: Process Versus Conformity." In *Human Behavior and Social Processes*, edited by A. Rose. Boston: Houghton Mifflin.

———. 1975. "Rule Learning as Role Learning: What an Interactive Theory of Roles Adds to the Theory of Social Norms." *International Journal of Critical Sociology* 1:52–73.

———. 1978. "The Role and the Person." *American Journal of Sociology* 84:1-23.

Turner, Ralph H., and Lewis Killian. 1972. *Collective Behavior*. Englewood Cliffs, N.J.: Prentice-Hall.

Unger, Kay, and Marsha B. Jacobson. 1978. "The Punitive Sex." *Human Behavior* 7:51–68.

Upcraft, M. Lee, John N. Gardner, and Associates. 1989. *The Freshman Year Experience.* San Francisco: Jossey-Bass.

Van den Berghe, Pierre L. 1970. *Academic Gamesmanship.* London: Abelard-Schuman.

Walum, Laurel Richardson. 1977. *The Dynamics of Sex and Gender: A Sociological Perspective.* Chicago: Rand McNally.

Ward, Kathryn, and Linda Grant. 1985. "The Feminist Critique and a Decade of Published Research in Sociology Journals." *Sociological Quarterly,* 26:140–57.

Weil, Peter. 1986. "Closing the Gender Gap in Health Care Management: A Comparison of Early Careers in Three Recent Cohorts." Paper presented to the American Sociological Association, New York.

Weiler, Kathleen. 1988. *Women Teaching for Change: Gender, Class and Power.* Boston: Bergin & Gary Publishers, Inc.

Weinstein, E., and P. Deutschberger. 1963. "Some Dimensions of Altercasting." *Sociometry* 26:454–66.

West, Candace. 1982. "Why Can't A Woman Be More Like A Man?" *Work and Occupations* 9:5–29.

West, Candace, and Don Zimmerman. 1983. "Small Insults: A Study in Interruptions in Cross-Sex Conversations Between Unacquainted Persons." In *Language, Gender, and Society,* edited by B. Thorne, C. Kramare, and N. Henley, 103–119. Rowley, MA: Newberry House.

Whipple, William. 1987. "Collaborative Learning: Recognizing it When We See It." *American Association for Higher Education Bulletin* 39:4–6.

Whyte, W. F. 1984. *Learning from the Field: A Guide from Experience.* Beverly Hills: Sage.

Wikler, Norma. 1973. "Freshman Survey." Unpublished paper, October, 1973.

———. 1976 "Sexism in the Classroom." Paper presented to the American Sociological Association, New York.

Williams, Sue Winkler, and John C. McCullers. 1983. "Personal Factors Related to Typicalness of Career and Success in Active Professional Women." *Psychology of Women Quarterly* 7:343–57.

Wilson, Kenneth R., and Linda A. Kraus. 1981. "Sexual Harassment in the

University." Paper presented at the annual meetings of the American Sociological Association, Toronto, Canada.

Wilson, Thomas P. 1970. "Conceptions of Interaction and Forms of Sociological Explanation." *American Sociological Review* 35:697–707.

Women's College Coalition. 1981. "Summary of Results: Study of Women's College Presidents and Teaching Faculty." Washington, D.C.: Women's College Coalition.

Women Students' Coalition. 1980. *The Quality of Women's Education at Harvard: A Survey of Sex Discrimination in the Graduate and Professional Schools*. Harvard University.

Wotruba, T. R., and P. L. Wright. 1974. "How to Develop a Teaching-Rating Instrument: A Research Approach." *Journal of Higher Education* 46:653–63.

Yogev, Sara. 1983. "Judging the Professional Woman: Changing Research, Changing Values." *Psychology of Women Quarterly* 7:219–34.

Author Index

Subject Index